'THE KNOTTY'

An Illustrated Survey of the North Staffordshire Railway

Basil Jeuda

Published by
Lightmoor Press

Front cover: Top, Class 0-6-2T No. 167.
Bottom, Normacot Station on the Stoke to Derby line circa 1905.   *Both Author's Collection*

Inside front cover: Map of the North Staffordshire Railway and canal system, indicating also the several areas where coal and minerals were mined; this appeared in the North Staffordshire Chamber of Commerce Year Book 1912.   *Hayward family collection*

Inside back cover: Advertisement for the North Staffordshire Railway and Trent & Mersey Canal that also appeared in the Year Book 1912.   *Hayward family collection*

Back cover: North Staffordshire Railway poster, *'Blackpool for Gorgeous Sights'*, Wilton Williams c1920.
City Museum and Art Gallery, Stoke on Trent

Leek station, Christmas 1905; 69 class 0-6-0 No 117 working a Churnet service from Macclesfield, has just left Nab Hill tunnel and is approaching the up platform. Note the up home signal in the background.   *Author's collection*

© Lightmoor Press and Basil Jeuda, 1996
Designed by Christine Pemberton and Neil Parkhouse

British Library Cataloguing-in-Publication Data.
A catalogue record for this book is
available from the British Library.

ISBN 1 899889 01 9

Published by Lightmoor Press
47-49 High Street, Lydney, Gloucestershire GL15 5DD

Page make up by Artytype, 5 The Marina, Harbour Road, Lydney, Gloucestershire GL15 4ET
Printed by APB Process Print, Bristol.

Uttoxeter c1910. A good close-up of the uniforms and headgear of the passenger guards and porters, whilst the anonymous driver looks on. The NSR Knot is clearly visible and the young porter, bottom left, is wearing a reefer jacket. Watch fobs are very much the order of the day. *Stevenson family collection*

ACKNOWLEDGEMENTS

This book had been in the preparation for many years, and I am grateful for the support and encouragement given to me by so many people; sadly some, such as the late and fondly remembered Jack Hollick, will not be able to share the enjoyment of it but I hope that I have been able to do justice, through the scholarship of Jack and many others, to the memory of the North Staffordshire Railway - an important part of the national railway system, whose 150th birthday is being celebrated in the summer of 1996.

I have endeavoured to use photographic and other material which has not been included in any of the excellent histories of the NSR and of some of its branch lines, and in books of NSR locomotives and rolling stock. Inevitably there has been a small amount of duplication, for which I apologise, but then only to highlight a particular feature of the NSR.

It is not possible, in a book of this type, to cover every aspect of the NSR's railway and canal network but the photographs and other illustrations attempt to portray a railway and canal system, the communities it served and a way of life that has long since gone.

Individual photographs are acknowledged and I thank all who have supported me in this way. I have relied heavily for research material from Allan Baker, George Chadwick, Christine Chester, Bernard Holland, the late Jack Hollick, the late Ken Hopkins, William Jack, Robert Keys, Claude Moreton, the Signalling Study Group, David Salt and Bill Thompson. I am grateful for the assistance I have received from the Cheshire Record Office, the City of Stoke on Trent Museum, the Derbyshire Record Office, Foxfield Railway, Hanley Reference Library, Keele University Library, the Public Record Office, the Staffordshire Record Office and the William Salt Library.

I would like to thank Diane Rendall, Tim Shuttleworth and Camera Five Four for their photographic support, Christine Pemberton for patiently processing and re-processing the text, and the Publishers for their enthusiasm in seeing my research reach a wider audience.

Finally I would wish to place on record how much I value the continued support of my wife, Laura, in my railway research.

Basil Jeuda
Macclesfield
February 1996

'THE KNOTTY'
CONTENTS

Historical Background . . . . page   4

Running Lines . . . . page   8

Stations & Goods Yards. . . . . page 28

Bridges, Buildings & Signalling . . . . page 46

Locomotives & Rolling Stock . . . . . . page 58

Employees . . . . page 70

Heavy Industry . . . . page 85

Canals. . . . . page 103

Miscellany . . . . page 116

Stoke on Trent, 23 September 1846.
The cutting of the first sod for the North Staffordshire Railway.

HISTORICAL BACKGROUND

The origins of the North Staffordshire Railway and the Pottery or Main Line from Macclesfield Hibel Road to Colwich, reside in the railway politics of the mid 1830s. Examination of any map of England reveals that the shortest and most direct route from Manchester to London follows a line that passes through Stockport, Macclesfield, Leek, Burton and Rugby. Whether this line should be constructed - and by whom - became a matter of great significance, not only to the local communities and the Potteries through which the line would pass, but also of vital importance to the major national railway interests that were emerging during the 1830s - the London and Birmingham Railway, the Grand Junction Railway and the Manchester and Birmingham Railway.

There was also pressure from those with business interests in Liverpool to ensure that an equally effective railway connection existed between Liverpool, the Midlands and London. With rival schemes emerging in Manchester it soon became clear that agreements and compromises between the various promoters would be essential. One of the compromises reached in 1839, between the MB&R and GJR, was for the GJR to drop its proposals to route its line southwards via the Potteries, instead of via Crewe.

The consequences were twofold; firstly the national railway system from the north west, through the Midlands to London, that has lasted down to the present day was thus settled and secondly, as an article from the *Illustrated London News* of that time describes, *'before the formation of the North Staffordshire Railway, a large tract of the country was wholly destitute of railway accommodation. Although it contains nearly half a million inhabitants and includes the manufacturing districts of the Potteries, Leek, Congleton and Macclesfield, and the towns of Uttoxeter, Stone, Cheadle, Newcastle-under-Lyme and Ashbourne, all of them centres of business for the agricultural population of the surrounding villages. No inconsiderable portion of this large tract also abounds in mineral wealth - lime, coal and iron being found in abundance'*.

Whilst the commercial potential for a railway system in the North Staffordshire area was apparent, it was not until 1845, when various different railway schemes, which

linked Crewe with Derby, Manchester with Derby, and Stoke with Colwich, all meeting local needs but fitting neatly into the emerging national network, were embodied in legislation coming before Parliament in the 1845/6 Session. Royal Assent was given to three separate NSR Acts on 26 June 1846. The Pottery Line was one of these, from Macclesfield to Colwich via Stoke, together with a branch line to Newcastle-under-Lyme and a line to Norton Bridge; a total length of 46 miles 46 chains of double track.

The line between Stoke and Norton Bridge opened on Monday 17 April 1848, with the journey time for the ten miles being half an hour; the journey time between Stoke and London Euston taking five hours. For a few months from April until 9 October 1848 there was a temporary station for Stoke at Whieldon Grove, a few hundred yards to the south.

With the abandonment in 1839 of the GJR's proposals to link Crewe with Stoke, there still remained a gap in the national railway system, namely the link between the newly emerging railway centre at Crewe with the manufacturing areas of Derby and the East Midlands. The Chartist agitation of the early 1840s produced both economic and political uncertainty and certain of the railway schemes that were promoted up to 1840 were put on hold for some years. Then Railway Mania set in during 1844 and 1845, with a large number of new railways being promoted and seeking finance. There were no fewer than twenty-four new lines proposed throughout the area between Macclesfield, Crewe, Stafford and Derby. One of the strategic lines under consideration was the Derby and Crewe Railway, which was aggressively backed by the GJR (merged in 1846 into the London and North Western Railway).

As part of the negotiated settlement between the NSR and the Derby and Crewe Railway on 25 November 1845, the two railway companies were amalgamated and agreed jointly to finance the construction of what later became the NSR. What was eventually to become the line linking Crewe with Derby and Burton was covered by part of the three Acts given Royal Assent on 26 June 1846 - the Act authorising the Pottery Line, covering the section from Crewe to Lawton Junction and from Harecastle to Stoke; the Act authorising the Harecastle and Sandbach line, covering the section from Harecastle to Lawton Junction; and the Act authorising the Churnet Valley line, covering the section from Stoke via Uttoxeter to Willington Junction and from Marston Junction to Burton on Trent. The section from Stoke to Burton opened on 7 August 1848, as far as Uttoxeter, and to Burton Junction on 11 September 1848, from Crewe to Harecastle and Stoke on 9 October 1848, and from Marston Junction to Willington Junction on 13 July 1849. Initially, on the Burton line, there were three trains a day each way, with the journey time for the 29½ miles being 1 hour 50 minutes.

By mid-July 1849, the framework of the NSR had been established and opened but was very much set within the national network, serving both passenger and freight needs. From then on, until the company was absorbed into the London, Midland and Scottish Railway on 1 July 1923, the development of the NSR took several forms.

Firstly, there was the linking of towns in the Potteries and its suburbs. The well known Loop Line, linking Etruria and Kidsgrove, but also connecting Shelton Iron & Steel Works to the Sneyd Colliery complex and Birchenwood Colliery. The Biddulph Valley and Leek lines linked Stoke on Trent with Congleton and Leek respectively, and also served the Biddulph Valley Iron Works and the Heath Collieries at Chatterley Whitfield and Biddulph. Similarly, the short Trentham Park branch provided access for visitors to Trentham Hall and the emerging suburb of Trentham.

Secondly, mineral lines were developed to serve the coal and ironstone reserves and their related iron and steelmaking works, mainly to the west of Stoke on Trent. These lines included the Audley line, the Chesterton line, the Apedale line, and the Talke and Pool Dam lines. Being primarily mineral lines, often passing through remote country areas, they were very profitable and were not viable for passenger traffic. It was only the Audley line, which connected several mining villages between Alsager and Newcastle, and the Caldon line, going to the lower Caldon Quarry, that eventually provided passenger services.

Thirdly there was the development of certain small lines linking important towns into the NSR network but well away from Stoke on Trent. An example was the Ashbourne branch, from Ashbourne to Rocester, providing access to Dovedale for Victorian excursionists and enabling Peak District limestone to go by rail to the Potteries, the Midlands and beyond. Similarly, the extension of the Caldon branch to Waterhouses provided a connection with the 2' 6" narrow gauge Leek and Manifold Valley Light Railway, known as the 'The Toy Railway', providing access for countless thousands of excursionists to the delights of the Manifold Valley and of the Peak District.

Fourthly, there was the acquisition or leasing by the NSR of certain lines originally promoted and developed by others. The Silverdale and Newcastle Railway, for example, was leased to the NSR by Ralph Sneyd on 31 August 1860, under a 999 year lease. Again, the 1866

Longton, Adderley Green and Bucknall Railway, which ran from Botteslow on the Biddulph Valley line to Normacot on the Derby line (3 miles 54 chains), was worked by the NSR and bought by them on 1 January 1895. The Cheadle Railway, initially from Creswell to Totmonslow (7 November 1892), and then to Cheadle (1 January 1901), was worked by the NSR from the outset and acquired by them from the Cheadle Railway, Mineral and Land Company Ltd with effect from 1 January 1907.

Fifthly, whilst the location of stations throughout the NSR operating era from 1848-1923 was mainly determined when individual lines opened, the NSR carried out a regular review of the need to build stations at new locations to meet local needs and social changes. On the Main Line, for example, Tunstall was opened in January 1864 (to be renamed Chatterley in October 1873), and Hixon on 15 December 1864. Stations that opened subsequently were at Great Haywood on 6 June 1887 and at Aston-by-Stone (a suburb of Stone) on 15 February 1902. On the Leek line, the new suburban station at Stockton Brook was opened in 1 July 1896. Leek Brook halt was opened in 1904 to serve the County Asylum at Cheddleton. With the emerging competition from trams, three halts were opened on the Main Line, principally for use by workmen and served by three steam railmotors that the NSR purchased from Beyer Peacock of Manchester. All three halts were opened on 1 May 1905, at Sideway (closed in May 1924), Mount Pleasant and Whieldon Road (both closed on 30 September 1918). Similarly, on the Market Drayton line on 1 May 1905, halts served by the railmotors were opened at Hartshill and Basford (closed 20 September 1926), Brampton (closed 2 April 1923), Liverpool Road (closed 2 March 1964), Knutton (closed 20 September 1926) and Crown Street (closed 7 June 1949).

Subsequent new stations on the Derby-Burton lines after the original opening reflected the development of the suburbs of Stoke and Burton. Fenton station opened on 1 August 1864 and was enlarged in 1879; Normacot opened on 1 November 1882, Horninglow opened on 1 August 1883, Meir on 12 May 1894, Rolleston on Dove on 1 November 1894 and Stretton and Clay Mills on 1 August 1901. A new station at Egginton Junction, jointly owned by the NSR and the Great Northern Railway, was opened on 1 July 1878, replacing the original NSR station; a new station was built at Uttoxeter, replacing the existing Bridge Street, Dove Bank and Junction stations, and opened on 1 October 1881.

On the Churnet Valley line, new stations that opened long after the line was built were at Denstone Crossing, to serve the College (1 August 1873), at Consall (3 March

1902) and at Rudyard Lake (1 May 1905), the latter to encourage golfers and fishermen.

Finally, there was the one 'joint' line, the Macclesfield, Bollington and Marple, which the NSR and the Manchester, Sheffield and Lincolnshire Railway financed jointly and equally; this line was of strategic importance to both companies - for the NSR providing better access to the industrial areas and parts of Yorkshire and Humberside, and for the MS&L better access to the industrial markets of the Potteries and West Midlands. The opening dates of some of the later passenger and goods lines are listed below to illustrate how the NSR expanded its passenger and goods services.

The line from Etruria to Earl Granville's iron works at Shelton opened for goods traffic on 10 June 1850 and for passenger traffic on 13 July 1864; the line from the iron works to Hanley opened for goods on 20 December 1861 and for passengers on 13 July 1864. The development of the Loop Line from Hanley, as far as Tunstall, occurred with the opening for passenger and goods traffic on 1 December 1873, to Goldenhill on 1 October 1874 and to Kidsgrove on 15 November 1875. The Grange branch opened for goods traffic on 29 March 1872, the Newfields branch for goods traffic on 1 October 1872 and the Pinnox branch for both goods and passenger traffic on 27 July 1892.

The line from Lawton Junction to Wheelock was opened for goods traffic on 21 January 1852, but it was not until 3 July 1893 that this was opened for passenger traffic. On 31 May 1852, the line from Rocester to Ashbourne was opened for both passenger and goods traffic.

The line from Newcastle Junction to Newcastle opened on 6 September 1852, for passenger and goods traffic, and for goods traffic to Knutton Junction on the same date; the passenger section to Knutton Junction in May 1863, and the passenger and goods section from Silverdale to Market Drayton on 1 February 1870. The complete section between Apedale Junction and Apedale opened for goods on 7 November 1853.

The Biddulph Valley line from Stoke to Congleton Upper Junction and to Brunswick Wharf opened for goods traffic on 28 August 1860 and for passenger traffic to the Upper Junction on 1 June 1864. The Leek line from Milton to Cheddleton (Leek Brook) Junction opened on 1 November 1867 for both passenger and goods traffic.

The Macclesfield Committee opened the Macclesfield, Bollington and Marple Railway for passenger traffic on 2 August 1869, from Marple Wharf Junction to a temporary station in Macclesfield and to Central station in Waters Green on 1 July 1873. Goods traffic commenced on 1 April 1871.

Turning now to the mineral lines west of Stoke, the Talke branch was opened in 1860 (leased by Ralph Sneyd in 1864 to the NSR and finally purchased by the NSR in 1904). The Chesterton branch opened in January 1866. The lines from Alsager to Honeywell Junction, together with the Bignall Hill and Jamage branches, all opened for goods traffic on 24 July 1870; the Audley line from Alsager to Honeywell Junction opened for passenger traffic on 28 June 1880. The mineral line to Bunker's Hill opened around 1884.

The line from Leek Brook Junction to Caldon Quarry and Waterhouses opened on 1 July 1905, though the first limestone trains from the Quarry did not start on it until December 1909. The NSR worked the narrow gauge railway from Waterhouses to Hulme End, although the line and rolling stock were owned by the separate Leek and Manifold Valley Light Railway. The last branch line to be built by the NSR was the Trentham Park branch, which opened for passengers and goods on 1 April 1910.

Stoke Station, 1849

The NSR was not just a railway system. It had its own locomotive, carriage and wagon building and repair workshops (employing at its peak probably around 900 people). It also owned hotels at Stoke (the North Stafford Hotel), at Leek (the Churnet Valley Hotel) and at Rudyard (the Hotel Rudyard). The North Stafford was without doubt the finest and best equipped hotel in the Potteries and, located facing Stoke station, was well placed (and still is) to meet the needs of travellers coming by rail and other means. Hotel Rudyard, originally the house occupied by the Lake's water bailiff, was enlarged between 1851 and 1906 to provide increased and enhanced accommodation for the growing number of excursionists attracted to Rudyard Lake. As part of attempts by the NSR to exploit commercially the attractions of Rudyard Lake (which, as a reservoir to feed the Caldon, and Trent and Mersey Canals, the company had acquired on 15 January 1847) the company sought to develop the Lake, Cliffe Park Hall and large estate which

it acquired in 1905, as a golf course and related leisure complex - employing the golf club professional and groundsmen for some years.

The NSR was a major canal owner and operator. This was brought about by the acquisition of the Trent and Mersey Canal from the Company of the Proprietors of the Navigation on 15 January 1847 for £1,170,000, thereby enabling the NSR to control its main competitor before any individual NSR railway lines had been built. In doing so the NSR not only acquired the Trent and Mersey Canal itself (93 miles 3 furlongs long and going from Derwent Mouth to Preston Brook), but also the Caldon Canal (17$\frac{1}{2}$ miles long and going from Etruria Wharf to Froghall Junction), the Leek Canal (3$\frac{1}{4}$ miles long and going from near Hazlehurst to Leek Basin), and the Uttoxeter Canal (13$\frac{1}{4}$ miles long from Froghall Junction to Uttoxeter). The Newcastle Canal (4 miles long from Stoke to Pool Dam Wharf) was acquired later by the NSR in 1863.

The Proprietors of the Navigation from the Trent to the Mersey in 1769 obtained a 999 year lease on a large tract of limestone at Caldon Low, located either side of the Stoke to Ashbourne road, and this interest, together with the 3' 6" tramway system from the Caldon Quarry to Froghall Basin, passed to the NSR in 1847; the LMS took over the lease on the 'grouping' of the NSR in July 1923, and in the depression of the early 1930s the lease was transferred to Messrs Hadfield of Sheffield, a subsidiary of the Derbyshire Stone Company. Between the early 1850s and the 1880s, output from the quarry expanded to over 200,000 tons annually. By 1902 there were over 300 NSR employees at the quarry, mostly paid at piece work rate.

Despite being surrounded by the major national railways, such as the L&NWR, the Great Western, the Midland and the Great Central Railways, the NSR sturdily maintained its independence and integrity and memories of it still live on in the minds of many today.

RUNNING LINES

Stockport Edgeley 20 April 1922; F class 0-6-4T No. 114 powers its way through on the middle road with the Manchester to London express.
National Railway Museum

Manchester London Road c1920, with K class 4-4-2T locomotive No. 39 at the head of a rake of L&NWR passenger stock, working the 12.05pm Manchester London Road to London Euston express. *Author's collection*

Poynton station c1910 looking north, with B class 2-4-0T locomotive No. 23 approaching the L&NWR station on a passenger working from Manchester London Road. Just to the right of the locomotive can be seen Poynton signal box, behind which was the line to Poynton Collieries, which had its own internal railway system. This was the second station at Poynton and was opened in 1887; the first was at Midway, a mile nearer to Macclesfield, which opened on 24 November 1845. *J Ryan collection*

Moss Bridge Congleton c1910, looking towards Congleton station, with B class 2-4-0T locomotive No. 26, working a local up passenger train to Stoke, its fine plume of smoke blending in with the wintry scene. Just visible in the background is a tall home signal and behind is Congleton signal box and station.
Author's collection

Harecastle station looking north c1905, with the line to Crewe, Sandbach and Audley to the left and the main line to Congleton and Macclesfield to the right. There is much to admire in this photograph, such as the lattice bridge which straddles four platforms and the two water columns, one in the centre of the picture and the other to the far right on the main line up platform. On the left can be seen some close-coupled passenger stock with a two compartment brake third at the end. On the up main line platform a fair number of station staff and three elegantly dressed Edwardian ladies can just be discerned.
R Keys collection

Harecastle station c1906, looking north with the line from Crewe on the left and the main line from Macclesfield on the right. The photograph is taken from a bridge over the Trent and Mersey Canal; Harecastle Tunnel is on the left but out of sight. Coming off the Crewe line is B class 2-4-0T locomotive No. 21, at the head of a local train of 4-wheel stock and 6-wheel stock, with a group of youngsters, perhaps train spotters, just visible beyond the steps. Harecastle Junction box can be seen on the left, cut into the bank, with the train framed by two tall home signals.
Author's collection

Stoke South Junction 30 June 1909, looking north, with the Stoke station down distant signals in the foreground and the up home signals, from left to right, the Colwich line, the Derby line and the Biddulph Valley line in the background The NSR locomotives on the left of the picture are thought to be an 0-6-0 2T DX or L class, behind which is an E class 0-6-0 tender locomotive. In the right foreground the first two wagons belong to the Midland Coal, Coke & Iron Co. Ltd. *Author's collection*

Stoke South Junction 30 June 1909, again looking north, with an unidentified L&NWR locomotive leaving Stoke station at the head of a Manchester to London express working. The locomotive is a four cylinder 4-4-0 Webb compound, either a 'Jubilee' or an 'Alfred the Great' class. Immediately behind is either a 45 or 50 foot Brake Van and a rake of L&NWR passenger stock. *Author's collection*

Stafford Colliery and Sideway c1905, with a London Euston to Manchester London Road express approaching the down home signal headed by a L&NWR 'Jubilee' 4-4-0. *Dow family collection*

Rounding the curve to Colwich and passing the up outer home signal c1920, is an up express to London powered by an unidentified L&NWR 4-4-0 'George the Fifth' class locomotive. *Manifold collection*

Great Haywood c1895, as the Manchester to London express working, headed by a L&NWR 2-2-2 tender locomotive 'Problem' class and 2-4-0 tender locomotive 'Jumbo' class, powers its way through. *Manifold collection*

Stafford station north end, Spring 1907, with B class 2-4-0T No. 18 waiting to leave on a local service for Stoke. On the left is an unidentified L&NWR 'Precursor', approaching the down through line. *Railway Magazine*

K class locomotive 4-4-0T No. 14, seen here at Smethwick c1914, at the head of a rake of L&NWR passenger stock - a rare photograph of an NSR locomotive working in the Birmingham area. *Author's collection*

Ashbourne station 1904. This was Ashbourne's second station, built to replace the original one, constructed at the time of the opening of the line from Rocester to Ashbourne on 29 May 1852. The opening of the L&NWR line from Ashbourne to Buxton necessitated the building of a new station with improved facilities to accommodate the increased volume of passenger, mineral and freight traffic to and from the NSR network on to the Buxton line. The Buxton line opened on 1 August 1899. The station was built to a standard L&NWR design, along with wooden buildings and wooden platforms. The Ashbourne No. 2 signal box and signals are also to a standard L&NWR design with bay platforms and shunting neck. On the down bay platform can be seen a short rake of L&NWR passenger stock. The station was jointly managed by the NSR and L&NWR under the Joint Station Agreement dated 30 June 1901.
Author's collection

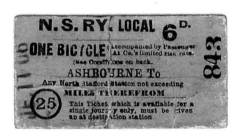

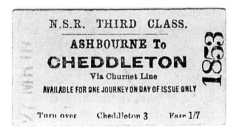

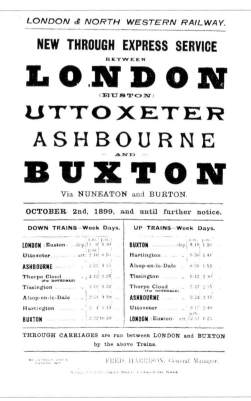

Rushton station 1905 looking towards Rudyard and Leek, with B class 2-4-0T locomotive at the head of the milk and passenger train destined for Manchester London Road, possibly the 'Froghall' milk. The elegant Jacobean design typical of nearly all the stations on the Churnet Valley line is clearly seen in this photograph. Beyond the train can just be discerned the Rushton signal box, opened in 1883, and the wooden goods shed. To the left of the station is *The Railway* public house, which was built around 1849 when the station opened. The sign advertising the receipt and dispatch of telegrams is clearly visible and for many years the station master was also the local postmaster. The centre of the photograph is dominated by the down home starter signal, whilst in the right foreground is a horse and milk dray, so typical of those used by the many local farmers who took their milk to the station.   *T Sumner collection*

Cheddleton station 1921, taken from the banks of the River Churnet, with D class 0-6-0T locomotive No. 132 at the head of a goods train. The private owner wagon behind the locomotive belongs to Foxfield Colliery. On the right can be seen the small 19-lever signal box and inside, just visible, is the porter-signalman. The design of the station building is identical to that of Rushton.

Author's collection

Consall 1910, looking north as a local passenger train, just visible in the background, departs Consall station for Froghall. In the foreground, left, are the station master's house and two other station houses built at the beginning of the year in time for the opening of the station on 3 March 1902; these houses were built on the site of former sidings, used in the 1860s and 1870s for the transhipment of ironstone which was mined extensively for a few miles on either side of the Churnet Valley between Consall and Froghall. Running parallel to the railway line between Cheddleton and Froghall is the Caldon Canal, part of which was diverted in 1847 and 1848 at Consall, during the construction of the railway line, to provide an easier route through the narrow valley for the railway. A narrow boat, used for transporting lime, is seen here being worked back empty to Froghall basin.   *R Poole collection*

Oakamoor Tunnel looking north c1905, with B class 2-4-0T locomotive No. 29 passing the Crossing House and the up home signal, as it approaches Oakamoor station with a three coach local passenger train destined for Uttoxeter and Derby. The line that veers to the right is the 'Wing' line to the copper and brass works of Thomas Bolton & Sons and to the brick works of Elijah Bottom & Sons. In the fork can be seen a ground signal, the bridge over the River Churnet and the cottages on 'The Island'.   *Author's collection*

Oakamoor station c1890, with B class 2-4-0 locomotive No. 29 at the head of some close-coupled 4-wheel and 6-wheel passenger stock on a passenger working to Leek and Macclesfield. This photograph was taken before improvements took place to the booking office and the northern end of the station building was extended in the early 1890s. *Author's collection*

Oakamoor station c1905, looking north towards Froghall, with B class 2-4-0T No. 21 at the head of a Churnet passenger train to which two horse boxes have been attached between the engine and the brake third. Permanent way material can be seen in the left foreground and cut timber lies to either side of the crane. Over the years, substantial amounts of timber, cut down from the wooded slopes of the Churnet Valley, were moved by rail from Oakamoor itself, Alton, Rocester and Clifton; Uttoxeter station had its own timber gang. On the down platform is the original stone signal box, which was replaced c1908 by a brick based timber signal box nearer to Oakamoor tunnel, visible in the background. *Manifold collection*

Burslem station c1913, looking towards Hanley with an unidentified tank locomotive about to depart for Tunstall hauling a loop line train of both 4- and 6-wheel carriages. The detail in this photograph is considerable; centre left is the McKenzie & Holland-built signal box and in the sidings nearest the platform are five Pyx wagons containing fairly small stone, one Clee Hill wagon containing coarser aggregate, one sheeted wagon and one high sided wagon at the far end holding crates. Cut timber is clearly visible as is the 5 ton crane. Next to the Midland Railway wagon is a Longbottom 3-plank open wagon with side doors and rounded ends, No. 4651, (rarely photographed). Other 3-plank wagons are to be seen in the yard and in the siding beyond the far platform. Behind the billowing smoke is the station master's house, built in 1891, whilst the main station buildings appear to the far right in the background, with the goods offices and stables to the right of the crane. The station opened on 1 November 1873.

Author's collection

Rocester station c1910, looking north towards Denstone and Alton, as a local passenger train comes off the Ashbourne branch and snakes past Rocester signal box. The token is handed over to the signalman when the single line section finishes. The tall signals at the end of the down platform are for the Churnet line (left) and for the Ashbourne line (right). Behind the signal gantry can be seen another gantry, used for lifting stone brought down from the nearby Hollington Quarries for cutting, prior to dispatch all over the country. Note the advertisements for Lipton's Tea and for Pears Soap, whilst in the bay platform on the right stand a 4-wheel milk van and 3rd class passenger stock. *Author's collection*

Shrewsbury 1920, with a 4-4-0T seen here fraternising with Great Western Railway locomotives against the backdrop of an L&NWR water column and signal gantry. *Manifold collection*

Crewe station 1910, looking north. D class 0-6-0T locomotive No. 125A is at the head of a local working to Stoke. This is a view taken from No. 5 bay, showing No. 6 bay with the platform behind. In the background can be seen a NSR tender.   *L Ward collection*

Crewe station c 1914 as New L class 0-6-2T locomotive No. 93 works stock into the North Stafford bay. *Author's collection*

Radway Green 29 July 1912, with E class 0-6-0 locomotive No. 106 working a Sideway to Crewe mineral train.
                    K Nunn collection

Harecastle station c1908 was an important junction as the station boards clearly indicate. One board announces 'Station for Kidsgrove' whilst another, in the background, advises 'Change for Congleton, Macclesfield, Audley and Sandbach Lines'. In the foreground can be seen a five compartment 3rd class coach, No. 327, one of around sixty to be built between 1891 and 1907. Next to it can be seen a five compartment composite coach No. 277, one of ten built between 1891 and 1905. Next to it is a four compartment composite, one of seven built between 1895 and 1907. The chimneys in the distance indicate the location of Birchenwood Colliery, whilst Kidsgrove itself provides the general background. *Author's collection*

Normacot station c1905, looking towards Stoke, with a B class 2-4-0T locomotive No. 25 at the head of a Loop Line train and about to turn back. In the background on the right can just be seen Normacot Junction signal box and the junction with the Longton Bucknall and Adderley Green railway. The Loop Line board can just be identified on the leading brake third. *Manifold collection*

Meir station c1916, looking north towards Normacot as a local passenger for Uttoxeter and Derby is seen leaving the 808 yard tunnel and approaching the up platform. The main station buildings are on the left and the later style NSR waiting room is on the right. Station Master Watters can just be seen on the right. Meir was typical of several stations on the Derby line, being opened many years after the line itself, in order to serve the expanding suburbs of the Potteries and other Staffordshire towns. *Watters family collection*

Blythe Bridge station c1905, looking towards Stoke, with A class 2-4-0T No. 8 seen here working a Derby local passenger train and the tall Blythe Bridge signal box in the background. An interesting architectural feature is the wooden waiting room on the right hand side, which forms part of the goods shed immediately behind. *Foxfield Railway Jack Hollick collection*

Uttoxeter station c1904, looking towards Derby, taken from the chimney of Bamford & Sons' Leighton Ironworks in the left foreground, with hay rakes awaiting dispatch on the right. In the centre of the picture, an unidentified NSR tender locomotive at the head of a Derby or Burton freight, carrying mainly beer barrels and hay rakes, approaches the bridge taking Bridge Street over the railway line. Pinfold Sidings, a busy marshalling yard, can be seen on the right. Beyond the bridge can be seen the roof of Uttoxeter West signal box and on the left the milk loading dock, normally worked by three horse shunters based at the station, with the milk factory of the Great Western & Metropolitan Dairies to the right. In the background the footbridge straddles all four platforms, with the Churnet Valley line to Rocester on the left and the line to Derby on the right. Beyond the station the newly built engine shed and coaling stage, opened in 1899 are visible.

Author's collection

Uttoxeter station 1908, looking east with D class 0-6-0T No. 139 working a train of 4-wheel and 6-wheel passenger stock either into or out of the down platform bay. Behind this train is a short rake of milk vans, including 6- and 4-wheel vehicles. On the Churnet up platform can just be seen another D class engine, No. 44, at the head of a rake of passenger stock. On the left is a four wheel milk van No. 315, which has an oil pot on the far end of its roof for the attendant's compartment. *Author's collection*

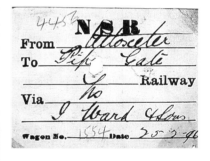

Uttoxeter station c1905, looking towards Stoke. It was an important junction station where passengers would change for Stoke, Stafford, Ashbourne, the Churnet Valley, Macclesfield and Buxton. The station was newly built in 1881 following the closure of Bridge Street, Dove Bank and Junction stations. The station design is identical to that used at the enlarged Fenton station, which was rebuilt and reopened in 1879. Passengers on the up line to Derby, on the right, are standing in front of the busy newspaper and book stall of W H Smith, one of several on the NSR network. *Author's collection*

Sudbury station c1905, looking east towards Tutbury with a complement of 14 station staff on the up platform. Behind them can be seen the original waiting shelter roof overhanging the platform. That on the down platform is of a later NSR design and had only recently replaced the original shelter, which overhung the platform in a dangerous manner. Note the up home signal attached to the station building and the signal box. In the background a train is departing for Derby. *Author's collection*

Tutbury station c1908, looking towards Derby. On the left, in the bay platform, is the passenger stock for the 'Tutbury Jenny', the passenger shuttle service between Tutbury and Burton. The belching smoke from Nestlés as ever dominates the skyline. Clearly visible is the tall up home signal, to the right of the chimney. The main station building is of a design not found elsewhere on the NSR network. In the background, to the right of the buildings, is one of two NSR police stations, the other being located at Longport. Note the NSR station gas lamp, and water column. *Author's collection*

Tutbury looking east c1920, with E class 0-6-0 locomotive No. 119 at the head of a mineral train passing the tall chimney of Nestlés milk factory, Note the neat coal stacks on the left and the ground signal on the right.
A G Ellis collection

Tutbury c1920 as New L class 0-6-2T locomotive No. 96 leaves the station on a Derby local. In the background can be seen the bottle banks of a glass works, the footbridge and the roof of the Tutbury Gates signal box, a McKenzie & Holland design. *L Ward collection*

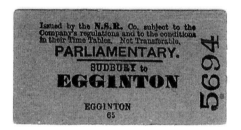

Egginton Junction station 1906, looking west towards Tutbury. The line in the foreground is the Great Northern Railway route to Derby Friargate. The station, jointly owned by the NSR and GNR, was built and opened on 1 July 1878, replacing an earlier one a mile nearer to Derby owned solely by the NSR. Behind the station building and running from right to left across the picture, is the NSR line from Stoke to Derby. Just visible beyond the white cattle dock on the left is the NSR waiting shelter on the down platform, in marked contrast to the more solid looking GNR designed waiting shelter on the right. *Author's collection*

Derby station 11 September 1923. New L class 0-6-2T locomotive No. 23 about to depart for Stoke.

H G W Household

Derby station c1912 with 19 class 2-4-0 locomotive No. 54 about to leave Platform 2 at the south end of the station on a Stoke service.

B Radford collection

Derby station west end on 29 December 1908. This delightful snowy scene shows the Midland Railway gantry and London Road Junction signal box, behind which and not visible was the NSR's two-road engine shed. It was located in the fork between the lines veering off to the left of the Midland Railway's Carriage & Wagon Works and the main line to London passing under London Road bridge in the background, centre. Just visible in the centre are workers, presumably cleaning points. On the far right is the St Andrews goods station of the L&NWR, which was itself used by the NSR. *Dow family collection*

Stretton & Clay Mills station c1902, looking towards Rolleston-on-Dove, has every appearance of a newly built station; it was opened on 1 January 1901. It reflected the final design used by the NSR for its smaller country stations, and identical facilities were built, for example, at Bradnop, Ipstones, Waterhouses and Rudyard Lake, all opened in 1905. *Author's collection*

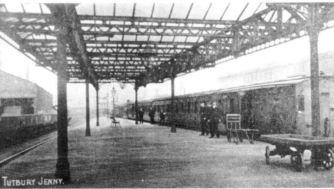

Burton-on-Trent station 1900, with the 'Tutbury Jenny' in the Bay platform at the north end, which was used by NSR trains. Beside the train is a Midland railway 2-wheel platform barrow, whilst the 4-wheel trolley is either of NSR or L&NWR design. The 'Tutbury Jenny' was the nickname for the service between Burton-on-Trent and Tutbury, a distance of $5^{1}/2$ miles, which was operated by the NSR using a tank locomotive and normally two or three non-corridor carriages, This shuttle service started in 1848 and lasted until 11 June 1960. *H N Twells collection*

STATIONS & GOODS YARDS

North Rode station c1920, looking north to Macclesfield. The station opened on 18 June 1849 with the rest of the line from Macclesfield to Congleton, at which point it connected with the line to Harecastle and Stoke. The waiting room on the left was modified because the original was lower and overhung the platform. The station building on the right was tall and imposing, out of all proportion to the population of North Rode which in 1851 numbered no more than 278. *Author's collection*

Mow Cop for Scholar Green station c1906, looking south towards Harecastle with the signal box on the right. The station, which opened on 9 October 1848, had staggered platforms, with the down platform for Congleton and Macclesfield located behind the photographer. On the left can be seen the kissing gates at the side of the level crossing and in the background the wooden platform extension of 1905. *B Morris collection*

Exterior, Stoke station 1897, the station being decorated with electric light bulbs for the 60th anniversary of Queen Victoria's accession to the throne. The station building dates from 1848; notice the lattice pattern brickwork at the first floor level.

City Museum Stoke-on-Trent collection

A view of the interior of Stoke station looking south c1880. Note the water column, the single through running line down the centre of the station and the lightly ballasted track. The signs on the left are clearly visible and include an outfitting room. A new roof and electric lighting facilities were completed by Handyside on 12 September 1895 and an additional through line was put in at the same time. *Author's collection*

The exterior of Trentham station in the summer of 1909, as a flycab awaits the arrival of passengers. The original station was opened on 17 April 1848 but was replaced in 1851 with a station designed by Sir Charles Barry to meet the wishes of the very prominent local landowner, the Duke of Sutherland. Observe the elegant pantile roofs.   *Newcastle Museum collection*

Weston & Ingestre station c1920, was opened on 1 May 1849 as Weston station, being renamed on 24 June 1885. On the left can just be seen the signal box, constructed to McKenzie & Holland design No. 1.   *Author's collection*

Great Haywood station looking towards Colwich c1904. This was a small country station which was opened for passenger traffic on 6 June 1887. It was of wooden construction of a design similar to that used on the Audley line as every attempt was made by the NSR to keep construction costs to a minimum. Note also the wide wooden platforms.

Author's collection

Colwich c1905, with the original station built by the Trent Valley Railway on the left - which still survives - and the L&NWR station building in the centre. Colwich was the most southerly outpost of the NSR. The Company had a one lane engine shed at Colwich, opened in 1851 and closed in 1896, although the turntable was kept in use until early post-grouping days for turning locomotives which were being 'run-in' between Stoke locomotive works and Colwich.

Author's collection

Norton Bridge c1905, looking south along the L&NWR line from Crewe to Stafford, with the station buildings on the down side. Norton Bridge was on the edge of the NSR network and the Company owned one house, used by its Goods Agent, and two other houses rented to coaching or signalling staff here.

Staffordshire County Council

Alsager station c1905, looking south towards Harecastle and Stoke. Note the distinctive columns supporting the roof which overhangs the up platform. The station opened on 9 October 1848 and its external appearance altered very little over the intervening years. Visible, centre left, is the well stocked book stall. In the foreground can be seen the wooden crossing for passengers which locals considered dangerous. They pressed, to no avail, for the erection of a footbridge or the building of a subway. On the right a porter's trolley waits for business.

Author's collection

Leigh station 1905, looking west. The stone features and tall chimneys were very much a feature of the first NSR stations; Leigh was opened on 7 August 1848. Beyond can be seen the small signal box. This country station was an important milk depot for nearby farmers and the Great Western & Metropolitan Dairies had a milk factory here, to the left but out of view.

Author's collection

Tean station 1907, with the newly constructed booking office replacing part of the original Totmonslow station, opened on 7 November 1892 by the Cheadle Railway. The NSR took over the Cheadle Railway with effect on 1 January 1907 and this resulted in the provision of improved station accommodation at both Tean and Cheadle; an existing building being transferred from Keele Park in March 1907, when that station closed, and was rebuilt at Tean in May 1907.

Author's collection

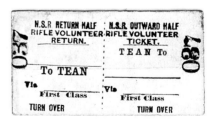

Milton station c1909, looking towards Stoke, with the acrid smoke of the British Aluminium Company Works, and the chemical works of Josiah Hardman Ltd, (served by sidings put in c1889), filling the sky. Centre foreground, is the timber framed booking office and waiting room and to the left, at the top of the path leading from the platform, stands the station master's house. Milton was opened on 1 November 1867 and the station and buildings were enlarged in 1880 and again in 1889. The Leek line was single from Milton Junction to Cheddleton Junction (Leek Brook Junction), a distance of 6 miles 46 chains. As a result of an increased volume of traffic, partly to the Manifold Valley and partly from Caldon Quarry, the doubled section from Leek Brook to Wall Grange was opened on 7 August 1909 and that from Wall Grange to Endon on 25 March 1910. *Author's collection*

Stockton Brook in 1917, with station master Hudson beside the timber framed building. This design was the one used in the 1890s and 1900s as the NSR opened new stations in country areas such as Ipstones, Bradnop and Rudyard Lake. Stockton Brook opened on 1 July 1896 in order to serve the expanding population that had moved into the many new houses being built in this pleasant Potteries suburb during the 1890s. Note the period advertising boards - for Veno's cough cure, Mazawatee tea, Teeton's of Hanley and Pears soap - and the Nestlé chocolate vending machine. *Author's collection*

Endon station c1910, looking towards Stockton Brook as a passenger train bound for Leek approaches to collect business commuters. The station opened for goods traffic on 1 July 1867 and for passengers on 1 November of that year. On the right stands the crossing keeper's house, typical of the NSR 1860s design, which could be found on the Biddulph Valley, Leek and Market Drayton lines.

S Hobson collection

Wall Grange station 1910, looking towards Leek with a train for there from Stoke about to depart and a large number of workmen walking along the platform. The main station building is on the right and next to the two little children in Edwardian dress is the outside ground frame. The Leek branch was opened for minerals traffic on 1 July 1867 and on 1 November 1867 for passengers. The photograph shows the results of the track doubling, with a new platform and waiting shelter in place. Smoke belches forth from the Staffordshire Potteries Water Board pumping station, whilst the Caldon Canal flows serenely past in the background.

Leek Post and Times

Market Drayton c1912, taken from the Adderley Road bridge. On the left can be seen Great Western Railway 0-6-0ST locomotive No. 678 about to depart at the head of a mixed freight, and, immediately to the right, is the bay platform used by the NSR. The passenger bridge across the track is to a standard GWR design and, in the foreground, is the GWR water column and home signal. A train of milk and cattle vans can be seen on the right, whilst in the background are the goods shed and cattle market.

Author's collection

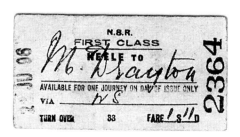

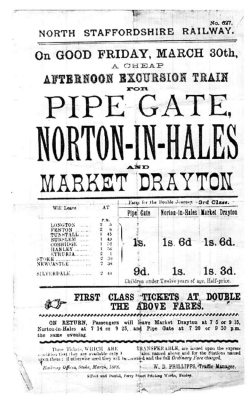

Ashbourne station c1890, looking towards Buxton. In the centre is the original station, opened on 31 May 1852, and to the left, in the foreground, is the station master's house. The glass canopy over the platforms (installed in 1877) can just be seen behind the low stone building with a triangular roof. The station was replaced with effect from 1 August 1899 by a new one nearer to the town centre and the market, on the opening of the L&NWR's line from Ashbourne to Buxton. The original station buildings continued in use for a further fifty years or so. The platforms were used for loading cattle traffic well into the 1930s and perhaps even later.

Author's collection

Clifton station c1905, consisted of a large collection of buildings in a very pleasant rural setting, close to the River Dove. In the background can just be seen the level crossing, protected by Clifton signal box, with its bow window, and an NSR 'kissing gate'. Immediately in front of the box stand the station buildings proper. Just visible are the signs for 'Telegrams' and 'To the Booking Office', the entrance to which is just to the right of station master Frederick Sherratt. The station master's house can be seen in the right foreground. Clifton station was built for the opening of the line in May 1852.

Author's collection

A 1903 view of Norbury and Ellaston, which opened on 31 May 1852 as Norbury station and was renamed on 16 July 1901. This view is looking towards Clifton and Ashbourne with the original station in the background. Of particular interest are the different height levels of the platform, with that in the foreground being lengthened in the autumn of 1900 to handle milk traffic. Behind the porters and station master can be seen the outside ground frame, which was replaced in 1904 by a signal box. Principal traffic from this station was milk and cattle, as well as timber, which required an 8-ton crane.

G Bowyer collection

Waterhouses station July 1905, looking towards Ashbourne with the standard gauge line in the foreground. Behind the station building and at a lower level is the 2' 6" narrow gauge line of the Leek and Manifold Valley Light Railway. All around can be seen signs of the new construction work - freshly laid and lightly ballasted track, new brick work and wooden fencing, the newly built station building, the gentlemen's toilet or 'earth closet' at the end of the platform and the newly built dry stone boundary wall. It opened on 1 July 1905. Note the station name board. 'Water-houses for Froghall Quarry'. By December 1905 a halt at Caldon Low was opened, which served Caldon quarry; the incline line to Froghall went from the quarry. The face of Brown End quarry can be seen in the background. *Author's collection*

Caldon Low Halt 1923, looking towards Waterhouses as the line descends on a 1 in 40 gradient. The halt was built to serve NSR quarry workers and other villagers in Caldon, a remote spot in the Staffordshire Moorlands. It was opened in December 1905 and passengers could join or alight on request. The Halt consisted of a third class wagon, seen here at the end of the short wooden platform. It was reached by a path across the fields. The tall, elegant NSR distant signal dominates the Halt. *J Plant collection*

Rudyard station 1897, looking north towards Rushton and Macclesfield, with the NSR owned Hotel Rudyard in the background, right. At this time Rudyard was a quiet country station catering for the needs of the local farming community and an increasing number of businessmen commuting into the Potteries; it also handled excursionists coming to enjoy the beautiful scenery on either side of Rudyard Lake. Features to observe are the station name board to an early NSR design, the narrow platforms and low canopy, and the open signal box. With the increasing commercialisation by the NSR of Rudyard Lake from 1905 onwards, the station was developed but soon became inadequate for the excursionist traffic of the Edwardian era. The main building was not to the design of the original contractors to the NSR; it was built and opened in mid-August 1850, approximately thirteen months after the Churnet Valley line opened in July 1849. *Author's collection*

Rudyard Lake station May 1905, looking south to Rudyard village and to Leek. The station was one of the last to be built by the Company and was located at the north end of the NSR-owned Rudyard Lake, which is seen in the background, lapping up to the station. The objective behind the erection of this station was to encourage excursionists from the Midlands, the Manchester area and the Potteries to fish, to go boating and to walk at the north end, as well as at the more popular southern end, of the Lake. The station also served the Rudyard Lake Golf Club, actively promoted and financially supported by the NSR, which opened on 19 April 1906. The station opened on 1 May 1905, in the charge of Foreman Warburton, seen here at the foot of the path leading down from the Rushton to Congleton road. This modest accommodation consisted of a Booking and Waiting Hall and Ladies Waiting Room, with a Gentlemen's Toilet at the end of the platform; an additional Waiting Room and Ladies' Toilet was later provided in 1907 on the up platform. *Author's collection*

Leek station 1921. A delightful view of this stone building taken from the station yard and looking towards Stoke. Note the elegance of the glass canopies, giving protection as they did for waiting cab drivers and passengers alike from some of the worst excesses of the Moorlands weather. On the right, in front of the advertisements for Stephens' inks and Hudson's soaps can be seen Sam Sigley's carriage waiting for business, and various NSR four-wheel barrows. On the far right, the door on the angle of the corner was the Parcels Office and beyond, in an alley, was the Telegraph cubicle for the public. Opposite this, and out of sight, was the weighing machine. The urinals were on the far left of the picture, then came the 2nd class and 1st class Ladies' Waiting Rooms and then the 1st class Gentlemen's Waiting Room. To the right of the archway leading to the up platform was the Porter's Office and the Booking Office. A sign for the NSR-owned Churnet Valley Hotel can just be seen in front of the trees in the background on the right, and the roof is just visible. *Warren family collection*

Denstone Crossing station 1907, looking towards Rocester with station master William Moreton on the up platform. This photograph should be compared with that on page 53, which shows the original and much larger crossing house. The original platform and foundations can be seen, as well as the platform extension which was built in the autumn of 1880, in advance of the remodelling of the station at the end of 1881. To the left of the station master is the lamp room, recently built in February 1903 and between that and the station buildings can just be seen the ground frame which worked the signals. Beyond the level crossing is the station master's house, built around 1880.
Staffordshire County Council (Shugborough) collection

Alton station c1905, looking south towards Denstone and Uttoxeter, with the station name board prominent in the centre. The station buildings are imposing, as befits a station serving the Earl of Shrewsbury and the many aristocratic guests visiting his seat at Alton Towers. Architectural features include the pantile roofs of the tall house belonging to the station master on the left and the Waiting Room and Booking Office just visible on the down platform on the right. Behind the porters can just be seen the signal box, enlarged in 1880, (note the decorated window boxes). In front of the bridge, is a goods hoist built in 1892 for the convenience of the Earl and his guests to lift their luggage from the platform to the road. Beyond the bridge can be seen an 8-ton crane and the goods yard, which apart from the local corn and coal traffic was heavily used for the movement of timber. *Author's collection*

Rushton goods yard c1905, looking eastwards to Buxton. Rushton was a busy goods station for corn and coal and had its own cattle dock. From left to right are the signal box, the back of the down waiting shelter, the goods shed, a NSR 8-ton van, three Sneyd Collieries private owner wagons and a rake of carriage stock parked in the bay. *Barks family collection*

Leek station yard 1913, looking north towards the passenger station. The construction of a new bridge and installation of new railway lines to serve the ever increasing traffic coming from Leek is underway on the left. Framed by the existing arch is the end of a private owner wagon which advertises Sneyd Collieries Ltd., manufacturers of glazed bricks. The original McKenzie & Holland signal box, built in the early 1870s, is about to be replaced by a larger, 40-lever box, as part of the expansion of railway facilities. On the far right can just be seen an unidentified D class tank shunting in the yard. *Manifold collection*

Rocester yard c1910, with two horse cart in front of a NSR 3-plank wagon and milk van. Rocester was a busy goods station for coal, corn, timber and stone, and this activity necessitated a 10-ton crane. *Author's collection*

Derby 1890, with the NSR engine shed and 46ft. turntable just visible on the left. The engine shed, with two lanes, was built around 1873 and closed as a NSR shed on grouping at 30 June 1923, though in 1925 there were 18 men and two 'Knotty' locomotives still stationed there. In 1909 there were 20 locomotives allocated between Derby and Burton NSR sheds, including one out-stationed at Colwick, two at Edge Hill and one at Longsight. By January 1918, Derby shed had an allocation of nine NSR locomotives. In the background can be seen the Derby Locomotive Works of the Midland Railway. The locomotive is a Johnson 4-4-0 tender No. 1320. In the foreground are two NSR 10-ton brake vans; No. 459 has two sidelights and a central vertical hanger type of brake arrangement, whilst No. 2091 has a single sidelight *National Railway Museum*

Congleton station and yard c1912, with K class 4-4-2T locomotive No. 39 awaiting the right of way at the head of the Manchester to London midday express. The station was opened on 9 October 1848. On the left is the tall McKenzie & Holland box, built in 1870, bearing the signal box and station name boards as well as the S&T diamond. In the foreground is the home starter and repeater signal, the elegant foot bridge erected in 1892, and the main station buildings with a lattice design in the brick work. In the background is the goods shed, in front of which can be seen a 10-ton van, a 3-plank wagon, and an 8-ton van piled high with beer barrels. On the far right is a 5-ton crane lifting timber, behind which can be seen the coal yard and an NSR house.

Author's collection

Ashbourne goods yard 26 June 1902, with the parish church of St Oswald, King and Martyr, dominating the skyline. This view is of the goods yard of the original Ashbourne station, and shows a block of coal weighing 2 tons 18 cwts from the Shipley collieries. This was for the Carnival procession of the Coronation festivities at Ashbourne on 26 June 1902. *Author's collection*

Brunswick Wharf Congleton, 1909, the terminus of the NSR's Biddulph Valley line. This is a charming view of a summer Sunday School procession passing the NSR goods depot in the background with its high brick walls. Also to be seen are the offices of William Hargreaves, coal, coke and lime merchants. The line to Brunswick Wharf opened for mineral traffic on 29 August 1860. *Author's collection*

Macclesfield c1910, with a delightful view of a horse and dray working out of the Macclesfield Hibel Road goods yard. Note the initials and the number 12 on the tarpaulin, an indication of the importance of horse transport for collecting and receiving goods, and clearly distinguishing the facilities provided by the L&NWR/NSR from those offered by the Macclesfield Committee, itself owned by the GCR/NSR. *J Hooley collection*

Macclesfield Hibel Road goods yard 1900, jointly owned by the NSR and the L&NWR, looking towards Waters Green. In the foreground is sawn timber and a 10 ton crane, with a L&NWR Guard's van in the background. Harold Poole is taking delivery of a consignment of timber which he had bought prior to delivery to George Roylance & Co. Ltd., joiners, builders and timber dealers. The huge dray horses were stabled in the yard next to the Roylance family house in Brock Street, in close proximity to the works.

Mrs K Dale collection

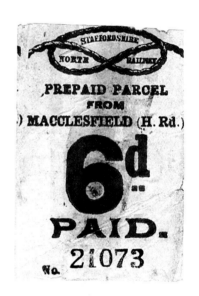

Poynton station c1908, looking northwards towards Middlewood and Marple, is of a NSR design also found on the Stoke to Market Drayton branch which was built at the same time, around 1869. Note that the postcard caption refers to Poynton as a 'GCR' or Great Central Railway station, although the Macclesfield, Bollington and Marple railway was jointly owned by the NSR and the GCR. Observe the McKenzie & Clunes signal box on the right, and the line that veers sharply down to the left to Anson pit, which was part of Poynton Collieries. Because of the confusion with the other Poynton station on the L&NWR, the MB&M station was renamed Higher Poynton in 1930.

Author's collection

Marple Rose Hill station c1908, looking north to Marple Wharf Junction, with the station master and other staff. The heading on the advertising hoardings is Great Central and North Staffordshire Railway and there are advertisements for Rudyard Lake and for holidays in Switzerland. Also to be seen is a Nestlé chocolate vending machine and an enamel advertisement for Epps's Cocoa.

Author's collection

LOWER HEYES MILL, MACCLESFIELD.

Lower Heyes Mill Macclesfield c1905. Although this evocative Edwardian postcard refers to Lower Heyes Mill - the mill in the background - the view provides one of the best scenes to have survived of the railway facilities in Macclesfield owned and operated by the Macclesfield Committee (a joint company owned by the NSR and the Great Central Railway) at the turn of the century. The photograph is taken from Beech Lane with Station Street running across the foreground. At the bottom of the photograph is one horse and dray loaded with beer barrels, whilst another three are at the side of the chute down which milk churns were sent direct to the down platform. In the centre, left, is the former MS&LR engine shed and to the right, the new GCR goods warehouse, built in 1899/1900. In front can be seen the carriage sidings. On the far right in the centre of the picture can just be seen the Macclesfield Exchange Sidings signal box. Bottom right is an L&NWR carriage on the up platform at Macclesfield Hibel Road station, which is just off the picture, right; behind this carriage is wooden fencing which separated the NSR/L&NWR goods yards from one belonging to the Macclesfield Committee.

Author's collection

BRIDGES, BUILDINGS & SIGNALLING

Audley line 1895; 65 chains from Keele Junction looking towards Leycett, with a trestle bridge straddling the deep cutting. Beyond the bridge on the right can just be seen the Leycett starter and home signals.   *British Rail*

North of Leycett station 1895. The Audley line crosses on a trestle bridge the line from Madeley Colliery to Harrison and Woodburn Colliery. Madeley Colliery is behind the photographer and through the arches of the bridge some dumb-buffered wagons can be seen.

British Rail

Leek Caldon & Waterhouses branch c1903, during construction. The **top** photograph was taken between Winkhill and Ipstones with spoil taken from the cuttings, perhaps at Caldon or Bradnop, clearly visible on the left. Note the lightly laid contractor's track in the foreground. The **bottom** photograph shows a typical accommodation bridge on this line, built using beautifully dressed local stone.

Manifold collection

Bolton Sidings signal box, 1920; view towards Cheadle with signalman Arthur Plant and porter Billy Bunce looking across. Note the new brickwork on the base of the box, which was opened in March 1918 on the site of the original box. In the background can be seen the Wire Refining mill opened in 1917. *Bunce family collection*

Cliffe Vale 1895, looking towards Etruria. The down Etruria splitting distant is visible under the bridge. The signal box is located by the original level crossing site and was built in 1879, where the short-lived Cliffe Vale station was situated. Cliffe Vale bridge was built after 1871, following a level crossing accident. Ground signals are visible in the foreground. *British Rail*

Stoke South Junction on 30 June 1909, looking south. The left up signal on the gantry is for the Leek line, the centre up signal for the Uttoxeter and Derby line, whilst the right hand up signal is for the main line to Stone, Norton Bridge and Colwich. Beneath are the yard signals. To the right can be seen the down distant signals, the one on the left being for Stoke station platform and through road and the one on the right being for Stoke goods yard. *Author's collection*

Leek Brook North box 1922, looking across to Wall Grange as the midday sun casts a shadow across the brick work yards The box was built c1910 as a 3rd class box, one of the last to be built on the NSR network. Charles Haywood is seen here, smartly turned out for the 6am-2pm shift. *Haywood family collection*

Alsager East Junction box c1905, was located at the junction of the Audley line and the Crewe to Derby line. In the 1912 classification of 148 NSR signal boxes it was one of the more important signal boxes on the NSR network and was classified behind Extra First Class (9 boxes) and First Class (19 boxes) as an Extra Second Class box, with signalmen earning a maximum weekly rate of pay of 30/- for a 10 hour day and a six day week. *Author's collection*

Near Milton station 1895, with the locomotive *Hardman* visible on the bridge. Josiah Hardman, the Milton chemical manufacturers, had this 0-4-0 ST locomotive bearing their name. Through the bridge can just be seen the Biddulph Valley line.   *British Rail*

Norbury Bridge 1907, spanning the River Dove, was on the branch of the NSR between Ashbourne and Rocester. The original timber bridge was constructed in 1851, the line opening for traffic on 26 May 1852. This new bridge was designed by NSR Chief Engineer G J Crosbie-Dawson, the material used being wrought iron. The centre span was composed of two bowstring lattice girders, 187' 6" long and 25' deep in the centre; the two end spans were composed of ordinary web girders, 124' 8" and 81' 7" respectively. The main girders rested on wrought iron caissons, 13' in diameter, which were sunk into the bed of the river and filled with cement and masonry. The contract was placed with Eastwood, Swingler & Co., Victoria and Railway Ironworks, Derby. The weight of the structure was about 670 tons and no less than 53,000 rivets had to be put in on site.   *Author's collection*

Dane Viaduct at North Rode took the NSR main line over the River Dane between Macclesfield and Congleton. It was arguably the longest and most impressive of all NSR viaducts and this print, taken from the *Illustrated London News*, captures the elegance of Victorian life and the pride in its engineering achievements. The viaduct opened on 18 June 1849, and was 1,275 feet in length with twenty arches, each with a span of 50 feet; it cost £100,000 to construct and involved 2,000 workmen. *Author's collection*

Church Street Stone c1905, showing the Railway Crossing House and cottages. This particular design of crossing house was arguably the most attractive of those built by the NSR; examples could also be found at Bosley, Oakamoor, Denstone, Lawton and Hassall Green, and several have survived to the present time. *Author's collection*

Wheelock station houses c1905. A view looking south towards Hassall Green and Lawton, of the last design used by the NSR. Whilst the branch opened on 21 January 1852 to Ettiley Heath and to Sandbach for goods only in December 1866, the passenger service commenced much later, with the opening of Wheelock and Sandbach station on on 3 July 1893. In the foreground is the milk chute, first used in May 1893. The station houses were authorised in 1902. The NSR was one of the most progressive pre-grouping railway companies in terms of providing houses for its employees, especially in rural areas where housing was difficult to find. At 31 December 1922 there were no fewer than 371 NSR houses occupied by NSR employees. *Author's collection*

Wheelock and Sandbach station c1920, looking north towards Ettiley Heath goods station and the town of Sandbach. In the foreground, left, is Wheelock signal box, its brick base cut into the embankment, with the small waiting shelter on the platform and, above, the cream and dark red brickwork of the station building itself. The first bridge carried the road from Sandbach to Crewe over the Wheelock branch, in front of which is clearly visible the home and repeater signal.
Author's collection

Abbey Crossing c 1905, with its delightful crossing house was at Abbey Hulton, on the Biddulph Valley line near Milton. It was built in 1859, in time for the opening of the line for goods traffic on 3 August 1859. *G Bowyer collection*

Denstone Crossing in the mid 1870s, looking south towards Rocester and Uttoxeter on the Churnet Valley line. This crossing house was built in 1849 for the opening of the line and was possibly the largest on the NSR network. In advance of the opening of Denstone College in October 1873, Denstone Crossing station opened on 1 August 1873 and the newly constructed platforms can be seen in the foreground. The crossing house was extensively altered and lowered in 1881/82 to provide a station and gatehouse. The station was renamed Denstone in 1923. *Author's collection*

Alton station down platform, no later than 1864, with Alton Castle towering over the Churnet Valley. This is possibly the earliest surviving photograph of NSR interest, and can be dated as the platform was extended to the road bridge and a flight of steps built up to the road early in 1865. Passengers were required, when joining or leaving trains towards Leek, to cross the railway track to reach the exit on the up platform. Note the earliest type of NSR station sign, which lasted until the turn of the century. The safety fencing was a feature of the station design when it opened on 13 June 1849. *Author's collection*

Alton station looking north c 1910; note the ornate barge boards of the signal box in the foreground. There is a contrast between it and the architectural styles on the down platform on the left; notably the original 1849 waiting shelter with pantile roof and the tall stone buildings on the right (which consisted of the booking office, waiting hall and station master's house). On the left is the bay platform and in the background can be seen the starter signals for both the bay and for the running line. In the 1912 classification of signal boxes, as part of the Conciliation Board negotiations of July 1912, Alton box was to be worked by a porter signalman in charge of a Block Instrument at a maximum weekly wage of 21/- per week for a 10 hour day and a six day week; it was a 30 lever box. *Author's collection*

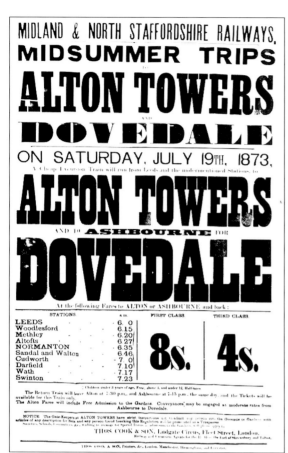

Caldon Junction 1923, with Caldon Quarry towering in the background. The line to the left is to Caldon Low Halt and to Waterhouses, descending on a gradient of 1 in 40, and drivers were advised to pin down the brakes of their trains. The line straight ahead is to the quarry, a distance of 1,067 yards, with Caldon Junction signal box, installed in 1905, tucked into the bank on the right hand side, having a very limited view of mineral trains leaving it; in the 1912 classification it was a 3rd class box worked by a porter signalman.

J Plant collection

Harecastle 1895, 37 chains north of Harecastle station and looking towards Lawton Junction. The bridge in the centre carries a tramway from Woodshutts' Colliery to a wharf on the Trent and Mersey Canal. Woodshutts was opened in 1803 and was part of a group which also included Harecastle, and Hollinswood. The locomotives were stationed at Harecastle Colliery. *British Rail*

North of Halmerend Sidings 1895, looking towards Halmerend station with the lines to the right going to Podmore Hall Colliery and Hayes Wood Colliery. The tall up and down signals dominate the skyline. *British Rail*

Pipe Gate signal box c1905, looking towards Market Drayton, was built in the summer of 1898 and was a 3rd class box on the NSR system. In the wage settlement of Conciliation Board 'C' on 26 July 1912, for a 3rd class box the minimum wage was set at 24/- and the maximum at 33/- per week, for a six day week, 10 hours per day. Note the unusual station design featured, with high platforms in the foreground, and at a lower (ground) level the waiting area in front of the station buildings and booking office. *Author's collection*

Railway Bridge Trentham 1914, showing views during and after construction. The view **top** looks north over the Newcastle to Stafford (A34) road, during the course of construction, whilst the view **bottom** shows the completed bridge. This bridge was a feature of the proposed Trentham, Newcastle-under-Lyme and Silverdale Light Railway, 5 miles 63 chains long, whose objective was to carry mineral trains from the Audley line clear of the bottle-neck at Stoke; its route was along the course of the Newcastle Canal until it connected with the NSR's Pool Dam branch. The proposals were delayed by the outbreak of the First World War, and as a result of altered traffic flows from the Audley line and of major proposals to remodel Stoke station, the Light Railway was abandoned in 1921. The bridge was designed by NSR Engineer G J Crosbie-Dawson and constructed and installed by Eastwood, Swingler & Co. Ltd. of Derby; it was never used but it was not until 1940 that it was demolished for scrap.   *Manifold collection*

Fenton Villa c1870, showing Robert Angus and his daughter in front of the NSR house built in 1866, at a cost of £400, for the Locomotive Foreman. Despite the apparent rural setting, the house was located due east of the Round House, facing the Engine Shed; High Street West passed behind the house. Robert Angus was Locomotive Foreman from 1847 to 1874, when the post was renamed Locomotive Superintendent and Angus became Superintendent for a year. *Manifold collection*

Bollington viaduct c1905, looking south. The MS&L in action as F1 class locomotive No. 596, a Parker designed 2-4-2T, built in 1891, is seen here working a Macclesfield Central to Manchester London Road service across Bollington viaduct. *Author's collection*

57

LOCOMOTIVES & ROLLING STOCK

0-6-0 Saddle Tank locomotive No. 56 or No. 57, seen here at the California Street Works of Kerr Stuart & Co. c1894. It was one of two locomotives supplied by Robert Stephenson & Co. to the NSR in 1862. They were withdrawn from service in March 1888 and sold in 1888 and 1889 to the Kidsgrove Iron & Steel Company.

Allan Baker collection

0-6-0 Goods Tender locomotive No. 89 c1895, was one of a group of six outside framed locomotives purchased from Neilson & Co. in 1865. They were all rebuilt between 1888 and 1891 and this particular locomotive was withdrawn from service in 1913.

Author's collection

Worcester Engine Company 1866-67. 0-6-0 Goods Tender engine No. 91 was one of a batch of ten built by the Worcester Engine Company for the NSR in 1866 and 1867. No. 91 was rebuilt in 1892 and 1904, before being withdrawn from service in February 1911. Note the neatly stacked coal in the background.

L&GRP collection

E Class 0-6-0 Goods Tender locomotives were a class of twenty-two built between 1871 and 1877, introduced by NSR locomotive superintendent Thomas Dodds. Whilst the first two locomotives were built at Stoke Works in 1871, the next ten were built by the Vulcan Foundry in 1872, then six by Beyer Peacock in 1874, with the remaining four built at Stoke Works between 1875 and 1877. The **top** photograph shows No. 111, originally built in 1872 by the Vulcan Foundry, in 1905 after being rebuilt, with brass numerals on the cab side; it also had rebuilds in 1888 and 1914. It was renumbered in LMS days, becoming 2330 in 1923 and 8657 in 1928, before being withdrawn from service in December 1928. The **bottom** photograph shows No. 66, originally built at Stoke Works in 1877 and rebuilt in 1894 and 1905. It was renumbered 2342 in 1923 and 8664 in 1928, before being withdrawn from service in November 1930.

Top: *L&GRP collection* Bottom: *Author's collection*

69 Class 0-6-0 Goods Tender Engine No. 115 was one of a class of eight purchased by the NSR from Sharp Stewart & Co. in 1873 and 1874. This particular locomotive was rebuilt in 1889 and 1910. After re-numbering as 115A in 1917 it was finally withdrawn from service in 1920. Note the bent weather board for the protection of the crew. *Author's collection*

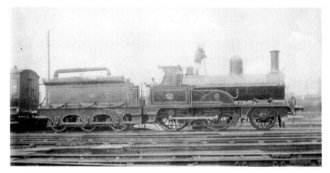

C Class 2-4-0 No. 15 was one of a class of five locomotives introduced by Thomas Dodds in 1874. The first two were built at Stoke Works in 1874 but the remaining three, including this particular locomotive, were built by Dübs & Co. in 1875. No. 15 was rebuilt in 1894 and withdrawn from service in 1906. *Author's collection*

Middle Right: 9 Class 2-4-0 Passenger Tank Locomotive No. 12 1874. With outside cylinders, No. 12 was one of three built by Sharp Stewart & Co in 1874 for the NSR, with a further two of its class being built at Stoke Works in the same year. They were required to work the passenger service on the Loop Line between Stoke, Tunstall and Kidsgrove, which was opened in 1874. This particular locomotive was rebuilt as a 2-4-2T in 1899 and renumbered 12A in 1908, before being withdrawn from service in 1916. Stoke shed can be seen in the background. *Author's collection*

Bottom Right: A Class 2-4-0 Passenger Tank locomotive No. 31A, seen here on 9 June 1919 outside the wooden breakdown train shed. This locomotive was one of class of eight locomotives designed by Clare and built at Stoke Works between 1878 and 1881 to operate the expanding local passenger services. It was renumbered 31A in 1914 and withdrawn from service in 1921. *LCGB collection*

ST Class 0-6-0 shunting locomotive No. 58 seen outside Stoke shed c1890, as originally turned out from Stoke Works in 1880. There were two of this class, the other being built in 1881. These locomotives were a familiar sight in the sidings and yards in the vicinity of the locomotive works at Stoke, where they spent the greater part of their working lives. Because of restricted height at the Newcastle goods yards, these two were for a long time the only NSR locomotives that could negotiate the entrance. They locomotives also worked occasionally at Froghall Wharf. *Author's collection*

ST Class 0-6-0 shunting locomotive No. 58A, the same locomotive as above, seen c1920 near the Round House. It was rebuilt in 1909 at Stoke and is seen here in Adams livery. It has been fitted with an extra footstep between the leading and middle wheels; the brake rodding gear has been repositioned on the outside of the wheels. It was renumbered 58A in 1899, as 1600 in LMS days and was withdrawn from service in June 1927.

Author's collection

B Class 2-4-0T locomotive on the turntable at Manchester London Road in the 1890s, one of seven of its class built at Stoke Works in 1882. 21 of this class were built between 1881 and 1895 and were used on suburban passenger working, for example, out of Stoke and on the Churnet line.

Author's collection

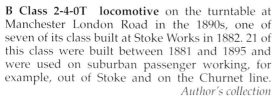

D Class 0-6-0 Goods Tank Locomotive, either No. 151 or 152, c1899. This photograph was taken shortly after it was built in 1898. Designed by locomotive superintendent Luke Longbottom, this class became the most numerous on the system, with all forty nine locomotives being built at Stoke Works, in every year from 1883 through to 1899. The locomotive is seen here in the Longbottom livery which was introduced in 1882. *Brassington family collection*

Erecting shop, Stoke Works, 30 September 1903, with rebuilt D class 0-6-0T No. 63, the second locomotive lined out in the new NSR livery. In late 1903, locomotive superintendent John Adams changed the main locomotive livery from Victoria Brown to Madder Lake. *Author's collection*

159 Class 0-6-0 Goods Tender Locomotive No. 164. Seen here in works grey, this was one of a batch of six built by Nasmyth Wilson in December 1900 to a Furness Railway design. These were powerful locomotives and generally used on coal and mineral trains, on long distance work to Rugby and on the Market Drayton branch. This particular locomotive was renumbered 2356 in 1923 and 8678 in 1928, before being withdrawn from service in March 1934. *Author's collection*

100 Class 0-6-0 Goods Tender Locomotive No. 80. This was one of a class of ten designed by locomotive superintendent Luke Longbottom and built between October 1896 and June 1907. They hauled long distance goods trains to Wellingborough, Colwick, Liverpool and Manchester. This particular locomotive was rebuilt in 1911 and in LMS days was renumbered 2345 in 1923 and 8667 in 1927, before being withdrawn from service in April 1929. *A G Ellis collection*

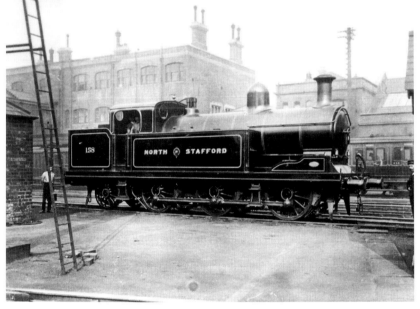

DX Class 0-6-2T No. 158 at the south end of Stoke station c1910. This class was the last tank locomotive to be designed by Luke Longbottom, and six were built between 1899 and 1902. These locomotives were powerful and with their large coal capacity proved extremely useful on the longer distance freight workings. This particular engine was renumbered as 2237 in LMS days and withdrawn from service in June 1929.

Author's collection

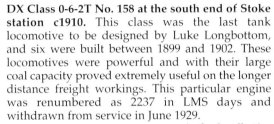

Steam Rail Motor No. 3 was one of three of its type, costing £2000 each and purchased from Beyer Peacock & Co. in 1905, in order to meet the growing competition of the time from electric street tramways which were financially subsidised by the local councils. The initial regular workings were between Trentham and Silverdale and no fewer than eight special halts were built for this service, which was mainly to serve workmen at very low fares; they also saw service on excursions, for example to Rudyard and to Hodnet in Shropshire. Beyer Peacock supplied the engine portion which consisted of an 0-2-2 tank, with the Electric Railway and Tramway Carriage Company of Preston constructing the coach section of the unit. In addition to forty 3rd class seats and six seats in a smoking compartment, there was a very small guards compartment which held light luggage. The Rail Motor was capable of reaching 30 mph and had high acceleration. All three Rail Motors retained their NSR livery after Grouping and were scrapped in June 1927. *Author's collection*

19 Class 2-4-0 Passenger Tender locomotive No.15 c1906, was one of a class of three built at Stoke Works in 1905 and 1906. Whilst they worked for some years on the Derby-Llandudno express, their 6' 6" driving wheels proved to be a disadvantage when working on shorter distance stopping trains on the NSR network. Eventually most of their time was spent on the Churnet Valley Line. This locomotive, together with the two others in the class, were all withdrawn from service in 1920 after a very short life. *Author's collection*

M Class 0-4-4 Passenger Tank locomotive No. 12 was introduced by John Adams in 1907 and was designed for short distance passenger work. It was one of a class of five, all built at Stoke Works between December 1907 and March 1908. This particular locomotive was renumbered in LMS days as 1433 and withdrawn from service in 1935. *Author's collection*

New L Class 0-6-2 Goods Tank locomotive No. 2 was almost the last locomotive to be built at Stoke Works. It was one of a batch of four completed in 1923 that was used on the system after the grouping, although the locomotives had NSR numbers and, other than No. 48, were painted in the full NSR livery. Although intended primarily to deal with freight traffic, this class proved to be ideal mixed-traffic locomotives, working goods and passenger trains all over the system. There were 28 locomotives in the class, the first being built in December 1908 and the last in 1923, and all saw reasonable service in the LMS days, the first being withdrawn from service in April 1934. Six were sold on, five to Manchester Collieries Ltd. in 1936 and 1937 (including No.2) and the sixth to the Longmoor Military Railway. No 2 is the only NSR steam locomotive to have survived and is part of the National Collection at the National Railway Museum; it is currently on loan to the Cheddleton Railway preservation centre. *Author's collection*

H Class 0-6-0 Goods Tender locomotive No. 92 at Stoke shed on 8th June 1919. This locomotive was one of a class designed by John Adams, the first batch of four being built at Stoke Works in December 1909 and a further batch of four built between December 1910 and March 1911. The H class locomotives regularly appeared on long distance goods trains, which the NSR ran beyond its own system, as well as on the midday L&NWR express from Manchester to London, which the NSR worked as far as Stoke. No. 92 was in the second batch, which had a new design of boiler and Belpaire firebox. It was renumbered 2366 in 1923 in LMS days and became No. 8688 in 1928, before being withdrawn from service in October 1930. *LCGB collection*

Near Stoke Engine shed, November 1911, with two locomotives both numbered 8. The locomotive on the left is K class 4-4-2T, one of a class of seven built at Stoke Works between November 1911 and September 1912, which were used by the NSR on the longer distance passenger workings from Macclesfield to Stafford and from Crewe to Derby. This particular locomotive was renumbered 2180 in 1923 and subsequently withdrawn from service in December 1933; all locomotives from this class were withdrawn by May 1935. The locomotive on the right is an A class 2-4-0T locomotive designed by C Clare, one of eight of a class all built at Stoke Works between 1878 and 1881. With the building of the K class locomotive on the left in November 1911, it was renumbered 8A and withdrawn from service in 1914. *Author's collection*

G Class 4-4-0 Passenger Tender locomotive No. 87, one of a class of four built in June and July 1910, designed by John Adams for the heavier passenger traffic on the Derby to Crewe line and for the through non-stop expresses which ran between Crewe and Llandudno Junction during the summer months. This locomotive was renumbered 596 in LMS days in 1923, and 5411 in 1928, before being withdrawn from service, after only nineteen years, in June 1929. *Author's collection*

KT Class 4-4-0 passenger tender locomotive No. 38 in immaculate condition at the Engine Shed, Stoke, behind which can be seen two loco coal wagons and the house of the locomotive superintendent. This is the tender version of the K class 4-4-2 tank locomotive and was the only one of its class. It was built at Stoke Works in 1912. In LMS days it was renumbered 599 in 1923 and 5414 in 1928, before being withdrawn from service in October 1928. Its principal duty was to work the expresses which ran in the summer from Derby and Burton to Llandudno, via Crewe.

Author's collection

New C Class 0-6-4 mixed traffic Tank locomotive No. 31 is seen at Stoke on 8 June 1919. This was designed by Adams for the most demanding mixed traffic on the NSR network. There were eight locomotives in this class, which were all built at Stoke between July 1914 and April 1915. This locomotive was built in July 1914, renumbered 2041 in 1923 and withdrawn from service in March 1935.

LCGB collection

New F Class 0-6-4 Passenger Tank locomotive No. 117 at Stoke on 25 February 1923. This was one of a class of eight designed by Adams shortly before his death in 1915. They were all built at Stoke between October 1916 and 1919 and on entering service they took over the haulage of the 12.05pm L&NWR express from Manchester London Road to London Euston, which NSR locomotives worked as far as Stoke; others of this class worked the Stoke to Manchester services and Stoke to Derby services. This locomotive was built in December 1916, renumbered 2051 in 1923 and withdrawn from service in November 1935.

W Potter

0-4-0 Battery Electric shunting locomotive No. 1 was built to the joint specification of John Hookham, the locomotive superintendent and Andrew Rock, the electrical engineer of the NSR. Built in 1917 it spent the whole of its working life on shunting duties at the Oakamoor Copper Works of Thomas Bolton & Sons. The electrical equipment, which was supplied by the D P Battery Company Ltd. of Bakewell, consisted of two motors, one per axle, of the BTH Company's GE pattern. Its driving wheels were 3' 1" diameter and its overall length was only 19' 8". It had a haulage capacity of ninety tons at 10 mph on the level. After nationalisation it was renumbered BEL 2 and, when the Copper Works and sidings were closed in 1963 it was withdrawn and placed in store. It was preserved at the Staffordshire County Council Museum at Shugborough for many years, before being moved to the National Railway Museum, where it now forms part of the National Collection.   *Author's collection*

KS Class 0-6-0 Goods Tank engine No. 75 was one of two of its class purchased in 1919 from Kerr, Stuart & Co., whose works were adjacent to those of the NSR at Stoke. They had been originally intended for service on a railway in the Argentine and one was featured in a Kerr Stuart promotional catalogue of the time. These locomotives were mainly used on shunting duties in Stoke yard. It was renumbered 1603 in LMS days and was sold in 1933 to the Nunnery Colliery, Sheffield, where it worked until 1953, when that colliery ceased to wind coal. It was then transferred to Handsworth Colliery, finally being withdrawn from service and cut up in April 1962.   *L Ward collection*

New M Class 0-4-4 Passenger Tank locomotive No. 17 was one of a class of four built at Stoke Works in 1920. These were a modification of the M class 0-4-4-T locomotive introduced by the NSR towards the end of 1907 and early 1908. The main difference was the length of the frames, thereby allowing for a larger coal bunker and water tank. This particular locomotive was renumbered 1439 in 1923 and was the first of the class to be withdrawn from service in 1931.   *Author's collection*

4 cylinder D Class 0-6-0T No. 23 at Stoke Roundhouse 1923. This was an experimental design by John Hookham for a locomotive to work the intensive suburban services of the NSR, especially over the severe gradients of the Loop Line between Etruria and Kidsgrove. It was the first tank locomotive in the country to have four cylinders. On completion, the engine was tested on a number of workings around Stoke and for this purpose was provided with a large indication shelter, seen here, which completely surrounded the front end. The results under the NSR were unsatisfactory and, following grouping on 1 July 1923, no further experiments were carried out. Eventually the locomotive went back to Stoke Works, where it was rebuilt as an 0-6-0 tender engine, coming back into service in March 1928 and withdrawn in December 1928. *Author's collection*

2-compartment brake third, seen here at Waterhouses, was converted from a 6-wheel brake van originally built in 1902. The family group add a delightful Edwardian touch to this close-up view. *Manifold collection*

3rd class 8 compartment third with arc roof, No. 110 was built at Stoke Works in May 1906. It was renumbered 14859 in LMS days, and 15256 after 1933; it was withdrawn from service in June 1940.
Foxfield Railway Jack Hollick collection

3rd class Saloon No. 143, built to Diagram 31 at Stoke Works in May 1909; Westinghouse-fitted, it had one lavatory and one large compartment seating 48. It was renumbered 14901 in LMS days and 964 after 1934 and was withdrawn from service in the first period of 1937. *Foxfield Railway Jack Hollick collection*

3rd class Saloon No. 290, built to Diagram 32 at Stoke Works in May 1909; also Westinghouse-fitted, it had two lavatories and a small luggage compartment and could seat 48. It was renumbered 14905 in LMS days, 966 after 1933 and was withdrawn from service in December 1940. *Foxfield Railway Jack Hollick collection*

EMPLOYEES

Uttoxeter Sidings 1894, with 0-6-0 goods tender engine No. 103, built by Kitson & Co. in 1853, providing the backdrop to Uttoxeter station staff. Seated left to right are; Henry Nuttall (dairyman), Tom Tucker (yardsman), ?, Inspector Snape, E G Wain (chief clerk), Henry Norris (goods agent), Joseph Beaman (clerk) and J B Grocott, E C Thorn, P Robson and H Allen (all junior clerks). Standing, 1st Row are; James Mellor (porter), ?, ?, Burgess (porter), Dick Fletcher (porter), George Rigby (fireman), Tom Walton (checker), George Wood (locomotive driver), ?, Will Lowndes (porter) and Geof Leadbetter (draughtsman). Back row; ?, ?, Sam Mellor (clerk), Frank Ward (clerk).

Thorn family collection

Passenger Guard 1890, with ornate bandolier. *Author's collection*

Passenger Guard c1900, wearing his reefer jacket, highly polished bandolier and money wallet, in a studio portrait.
Author's collection

Norbury & Ellaston station c1908, looking towards Rocester, with driver, fireman, goods guard and shunter posing in front of D class 0-6-0T locomotive No. 131. On the platform can be seen a porter and young lad with a single line token around his neck. Norbury & Ellaston provided a passing point for the single line working between Rocester and Clifton stations; the line in the foreground is the passing line. Behind the locomotive is an 8 ton van, a private owner wagon of Joseph Welch, (coal merchants of Macclesfield), whilst a high sided coal wagon can be seen in front of the home starter signal for Rocester. *Author's collection*

Stoke Round House 1896, with driver, fireman and cleaners in front of a newly built 100 class 0-6-0 tender locomotive, freshly out of the shops. The Round House is just visible in the background. *Manifold collection*

Alfred Bostock, Rushton 1906, immaculately dressed as a porter with shiny shoes, stiff collar and dapper bow tie. *Bostock family collection*

Etruria Station c1910, looking south towards Stoke. The young porter is leaning on a weighing machine, owned by the British Automatic Company Ltd., of Apollo Street, London. To the right can be seen the gated siding into Wenger's pottery works. The station opened on 9 October 1848 and later, in 1877, alterations to it and to the main line were approved, leading to the construction of the island platform which is seen here. *Author's collection*

'Peg Leg' Johnson, seen here outside Bolton's Siding signal box, Froghall c1908, where he worked for many years following a railway accident at Burton in 1872, in which he lost his legs. This was the original box, provided in 1890 when Thomas Bolton & Sons built their works just north of Froghall station. The box was replaced in March 1918 by a larger one on the same location, to handle the increasing volume of traffic from the expanding work-shops at Bolton's.

Author's collection

Macclesfield Exchange sidings October 1904, looking south towards Macclesfield with Thomas Baskville (left) and fireman N Eccles (right) on the footplate of L class 0-6-2T locomotive No. 124, acquired from Vulcan Foundry in November 1903, when it was given the number 170. *J Lake*

Froghall Wharf 1917, outside the office of the goods agent. From left to right are Primrose Thorley (owner-manager of the firm Thorley & Bowers of Froghall Wharf, lime burners), J T Alcock (NSR goods agent), George Henry Shaw (chief clerk), Ernest Ratcliffe (goods agent) and Edgar Hall (senior clerk). In the background are the Byelaws and Regulations of the Canal from the Trent to the Mersey, which also covered the Caldon Canal. Note the lime on the boots of 'Prim' Thorley and the protected toes on the footwear of the two porters. Sappho the dog used to run alongside the pony and trap of 'Prim' Thorley, all the way from Cheadle to the Basin.

Shaw family collection

Station master, as yet unidentified, at an unknown location. Nonetheless, an excellent close up view of a 'servant' of the NSR in his uniform and cap.

Author's collection

Crossing House Milton 1905, just north of Milton Junction on the Biddulph Valley line. This house, of an early NSR design, was built in 1859 on the opening of the line where it crossed the Milton road but the later construction of a bridge rendered the actual crossing obsolete. Here, Matthew Heath, platelayer and later signalman at the Milton Junction box, poses with his family outside the house, which he rented from the NSR at a weekly rate of two shillings. *Ibbs family collection*

Stoke Round House 1922, with cleaners, firemen and drivers clambering on board a D class locomotive with a further class member in the background. The shed for the Breakdown Van is on the right. *Manifold collection*

Stoke station porters c1910. There is a fine array of enamel advertising signs in the background and just visible is a Midland Railway notice.

Author's collection

Normacot station c1905, looking towards Longton with station master, clerk and porters on the down platform. This station opened much later, in 1882, than nearly all the others on the line from Stoke to Derby. It was opened to serve the expanding suburbs of the Potteries towns. The imposing house in the background was the station master's. Beyond is the station building with its unusual timber framed design, only found elsewhere on the NSR network at Horninglow station, Burton, which opened around the same time on 1 August 1883.

Author's collection

Ambulance team 1922, probably at Stoke Locomotive shed, with first aid box and stretcher in the foreground. The St John's Ambulance Association organised First Aid and re-examination classes every year at different locations on the NSR network. There would normally be a course of five lectures, though extra lectures would be given from time to time; re-examination also took place, but not at every centre. The courses were held at Longport, Stoke Loco, Stoke, Stoke Engineers, Congleton, Macclesfield, Newcastle, Alsager, Crewe, Burton, Caldon, Cresswell and Blythe Bridge, and class sizes ranged from 15 to 30. Lectures were given by one local doctor and the examinations supervised by another. The examination passes were graded - Certificate, Voucher, Medallion and Label. *Author's collection*

Barlaston station master, Mr Peacock 1917, in a studio portrait. *Author's collection*

Leek Brook North signal box early 1922, showing Charles Haywood working the box. A rare interior view of the block instruments and levers. This was a Grade 3 cabin (after the 1919 NSR reclassification) where the signal man received a weekly wage of 66/-. This was reduced on May 1 1922 to 58/- per week and to 51/- per week on July 1 1923 as part of a systematic reduction in wage rates from 1921, after there had been a substantial increase following the end of the First World War. *C Haywood collection*

Norton Bridge c1923. Two views of Walter Reader, **above** sitting by a NSR wheel barrow and **below** standing by his horse, with the L&NWR goods shed on the right and the NSR signal box in the background. Mr Reader began his railway career as a drayman on the L&NWR at a weekly wage of £1 per week; he later left that company and became a drayman with the NSR at a slightly higher wage of £1- 0s-5d per week. His job entailed taking two dray loads a day from Norton Bridge to Eccleshall, a distance of two miles. The loads consisted of all kinds of commodities, often including food, beer and spirits, which were conveyed in wooden barrels. *L W Reader collection*

Stockton Brook station 1918; station master Hudson and family pose on the wide platform, with the waiting shelter in the background. *Author's collection*

Round House, Stoke, May 1921. In the centre are a pair of driving wheels. Note the well coaled bunkers in the background, an L class on the left and probably a new C class or new F class in the centre. *Manifold collection*

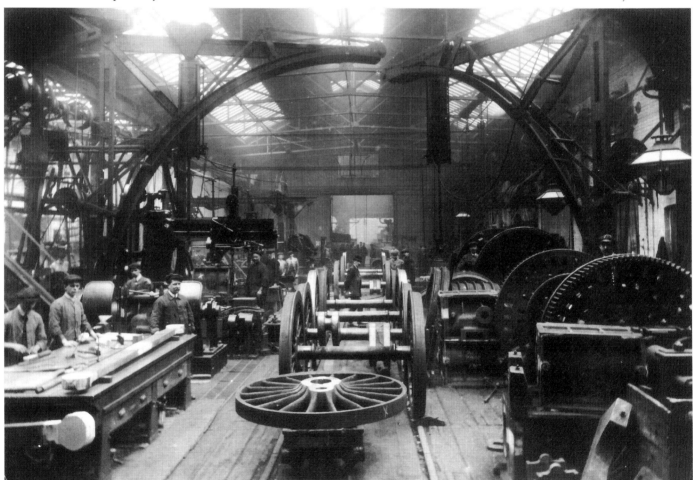

Main Avenue in the machine shop of the Locomotive Works at Stoke 1913, showing pneumatic hoists in the foreground and looking north towards the boiler shop. The Locomotive Carriage and Wagon Works of the NSR started in the second half of 1859; before that date repair work had been contracted to Joseph Wright of Birmingham, who rented the workshop from the NSR. The first carriage was built in the first half of 1861 at a cost of £195. Erecting and boiler shops were established in the first half of 1865 and the first locomotive to be constructed was in 1868; in all, 194 locomotives were built at Stoke Works. There was a major expansion of the Carriage and Wagon works in 1875 and by April 1879 there were 300 employees in this section alone. In November 1913, 483 men were employed in the Locomotive shops and 391 in the Carriage and Wagon works. *Manifold collection*

Six compartment First Class Carriage No. 284, on the left and Five compartment Composite Carriage No 271 on the right, in the Carriage Shop in May 1921. The First Class carriage with the elliptical roof was one of three built between 1913 and 1921, whilst the Composite, which was built in 1899, was one of ten built between 1891 and 1905. Behind the Composite is a further bogie carriage.

Author's collection

NSR two ton Lurry or Dray No. 159, undergoing repair in the Wagon Shop. The Lurry contains a plate 'H Ry 91/137' which seems to imply that the Wagon Shop was carrying out repair work for the Highland Railway. The notice board on the right contains details of the jobs passing through the shop, including 'H Ry 91/222'.
Author's collection

Part of the Machine Shop 1913, with foreman Robert Kerr in front and a further 25 machinists and two apprentices behind him, seen here in very cramped working conditions. In the foreground are several big centre lathes and lathe shafts, whilst centre right a milling machine is just visible.

Author's collection

The Smithy, Stoke Works 1913, was approximately 77 yards long and 15 yards wide. It contained two Ross-Rigby steam hammers, one being a 15 cwt forge hammer for heavy work and the other a 12½ cwt. The forge hammer was served by its own coal furnace, whilst other hammers were served by ordinary smiths' hearths. Elsewhere in the smithy was a coal furnace, a new oil furnace, two blowers supplying blast, two hydraulic presses, a buckling and testing machine for springs, and buffing and grinding machines, as well as pneumatic cranes, lifts and hoists. John Hookham, then Works Manager in the Locomotive Department, can be seen standing at the front on the right.

Manifold collection

Stoke Works Upholsterers or Finishers, Carriage and Wagon Department c1920. Back row, left to right; Haines,Rowling,Thomas Salt, Lancelot, ?, and Front row, ?, Goodwin, Booth, ?.
A Salt collection

Stoke Works at the turn of the century, with what appears to be an experimental motorised cycle. Third from the left is Peter Abberley, who worked in the locomotive section of the Works.
John Abberley collection

Stoke Works c1921, with various foremen and pupils in front of a D class locomotive. Second from the left on the back row is Clifford Watkin, who entered the Works as a pupil in September 1917 for five years. During this period he gained experience in three Departments. In the Locomotive Works he worked in Turning, Fitting, Erecting, Tool Room, Pattern Shop, Drawing Office, Brass Foundry, Millwrights' and also with the Water & Outside Department. In the Running Department he worked in Fitting and Inspection, and, in the Carriage and Wagon Department, in Inspection.   *Watkin family collection*

Uniforms of the NSR are illustrated here by **left** Fireman Billy Meir and driver A G Brook in front of 0-6-0ST No. 59A and **right** Billy Meir again, with shunter Clarke.   *Foxfield Railway Jack Hollick collection*

HEAVY INDUSTRY

Alsager c1910, with Alsager East box in the background. This locomotive was one of the earliest L&NWR 2-4-0T's, designed by Trevithick and built at Crewe Works in November 1852 as *Penmaenmawr* No. 295. It saw service on the Newcastle and Carlisle railway from 1857 and was converted to a side tank in 1870. For many years it worked on the L&NWR's Cromford and High Peak railway, before being sold to Joel Settle, coal factor of Alsager, in 1903.   *Author's collection*

Malkin's Bank, alkali works of Brunner Mond & Co. Ltd. in the early part of 1923, was one of several chemical works on the Wheelock branch. Whilst this branch carried only a small amount of passenger traffic during the relatively short time (3 July 1893 to 28 September 1930) when there were passenger services, it was an important freight line, carrying coal and limestone ever since it opened, on 21 January 1852, from Lawton Junction as far as Ettiley Heath. The Malkin's Bank works was located between Wheelock and Hassall Green and the running line is between the two NSR home signals. In the sidings can be seen 3-plank NSR wagons containing limestone; wagons from many of the prominent pre-grouping railways can be seen, the Great Western, the Great Central, the Great Northern, the London & North Western and the Midland, plus a lone freshly painted London Midland & Scottish Railway wagon. Sneyd Colliery and Settle Speakman wagons can be seen centre right.   *Cheshire Record Office*

Bunkers Hill Colliery c1905, looking south, was one of several in the area owned by William Rigby. It was located at Butt Lane, near Talke, and was originally served by a narrow gauge tramway to the Trent & Mersey Canal at Lawton; some of its course can still be traced today. Later, in 1885, a standard gauge branch was built to connect with the NSR Audley line. The Settle wagons would doubtless be taking coal to Rigby's washer at Jamage. Settle was a prominent local coal factor, and owned one of the first mechanised coal washing plants in the area, on the Jamage Colliery site near Red Street. This pit largely closed in 1915 and the branch railway was lifted but limited operation continued until 1919. *Author's collection*

Diglake Colliery c1905 at Bignall End, near Audley, was owned by William Rigby & Co. and dated from the middle of the last century. This colliery was served by the Bignall Hill branch of the NSR Audley line and was the scene of one of North Staffordshire's worst mining disasters when, on 14 January 1895, 75 men and boys were trapped by a large inrush of underground water from earlier workings; only two bodies were recovered. The pit never again made a significant contribution and closed during the First World War. In August 1933, miners from the adjacent Rookery Colliery broke into the old Diglake 10ft workings and three more bodies were recovered but it was decided to leave the remainder where they were in their underground tomb. It was, however, established that they had died from asphyxiation, rather than drowning. *Warham family collection*

Jamage Colliery c1905, a view looking south. Notice the NSR D tank lurking in the sidings, and the selection of private owner wagons. Those of Philip Speakman, a Liverpool coal factor, and subsequent partner with Joel Settle in Settle, Speakman & Company, are notable - their Company later owned this pit. Jamage and Jamage Main, off the picture to the left, were served by the Jamage branch from the NSR Audley line, opened in July 1870. The colliery shown here closed in 1941; however, surface operations survived until 1947, to serve the adjacent Rookery Colliery, the coal from Rookery being brought here for screening, washing and onward transmission by the main line railway.

Author's collection

Silverdale Iron Works, said to be taken in the 1860s and, so far as is known, the oldest photograph of the site. The view looks south east, and is taken from almost the extreme end of the Silverdale Tramway, which made an end on connection with Ralph Sneyd's Silverdale & Newcastle-under-Lyme Railway, itself in the distance. The blast furnaces and their blowing engine house are to the left, and the forges and mills to the right in this view. Silverdale village is in the middle distance.

W J Thompson collection

Silverdale Colliery looking north c1903, showing Kents Lane No. 17 pit of the Silverdale Company, very soon after the Butterley Company of Derbyshire terminated their lease of the Silverdale Estate in 1903. This was an ironstone mine; notice the men in the area between the pit and the sidings calcining the ironstone and then hand loading it into railway wagons - some of these are dumb buffered. Note also the discarded engine flywheel. The railway line in the immediate foreground is part of the original Silverdale & Newcastle Railway, dating from 1849-50 and one of the oldest railway lines in North Staffordshire. *Newcastle-under-Lyme Museum*

Knutton, an 0-4-0 saddle tank locomotive built in Scotland by Andrew Barclay Sons & Company Ltd. of Kilmarnock in 1900 - maker's number 882. This was a standard product of the builder, and came new to the Knutton Iron and Steel Works at Knutton Forge, situated where the Pool Dam branch left the NSR line to Market Drayton. The branch here and the main line towards Silverdale were part of Sneyd's original Silverdale & Newcastle-under-Lyme Railway of 1849-50. This works was a subsidiary company of the Midland complex at Apedale. *Knutton* was sold in 1915, (shunting thereafter being undertaken by a locomotive sent daily from Apedale), going north to the Cowpen Coal Company at Combois in Northumberland. *Allan Baker collection*

Apedale Furnaces, possibly taken as early as the mid-1860s, and well before the hot blast system was introduced in 1894, mechanical charging being added at the same time. The view looks due south, the pig beds lying to the left and the slag bank, or part of it, beyond. In the foreground can be seen a part of Gresley's Canal, dating from about 1776, the first man-made waterway in the area, built by the land owner, Sir Nigel Bower Gresley, to connect the Apedale collieries with Newcastle-under-Lyme; it was three miles long. This canal passed out of use about the time that the NSR Apedale branch opened in 1853 but sections of it remained until recent times. *Warham family collection*

By-Product Plant, Apedale c1915, looking north, was part of the large Midland Coal, Coke & Iron complex here. This is the By-Product Recovery Plant, and beyond it can be seen the coke ovens. These ovens produced coal gas to heat the blast furnaces, as well as coke for the iron smelting process. The By-Product plant served to distil all the other multifarious products of the coking process of coal. The railway line in the foreground is the 'Main Line' of the Midland complex. It ran from the termination of the NSR Apedale branch, right through the Apedale estate, and then extended to serve the Companies nearby Podmore Hall Estate at Halmerend too. There it again made connection with the NSR, this time the Audley line. The colliery headgears seen in the left distance are those of Burley Pit, the main coal drawing shaft on the site. *Author's collection*

Apedale Furnaces c1910, a view looking west and towards Halmerend. Of the six blast furnaces, the two on the left are out of use and, as can be seen, had never been modernised, adapted for hot blast, or fitted with mechanical charging gear - note the hot blast stoves for the other four furnaces behind. In the foreground can be seen the pig beds, where the molten iron was poured to form pigs, so called because the pig beds running off the main pouring channels resembled piglets suckling a sow! The blowing engine house is behind the chimney, and the building to its left is the then almost new power house, built to serve the electrical needs of the entire site.

Author's collection

Holditch Colliery c1916 was sunk by the Wrexham-based Brymbo Steel Company, principally for ironstone to serve their blast furnaces at Brymbo. There were two shafts, No. 1 sunk in 1916 and No. 2 sunk in 1912. The two main seams were Great Row and Four Feet. In 1930, following financial problems with its parent company, the colliery was sold to the local Shelton Iron, Steel & Coal Company, and gradually fine grade coking coal replaced ironstone as its staple production. Served by a line from the NSR Apedale branch, it provided the last traffic on this section, and closed in August 1989 - it was always known locally as Brymbo Colliery.

Author's collection

Talk o'th Hill Colliery c1923, showing coke ovens and by-product plant, was a sizable undertaking. Mining on the site dated from the early part of the 19th century, with the coke ovens and by-product plant dating from 1897. Earlier there had also been blast furnaces on the site. The Talke site was connected with the NSR main line at Chatterley by one of the earliest stretches of industrial railway in the area, needing an Act of Parliament, (albeit only to allow it to cross Turnpike and public roads) - 'Mr Sneyd's Railway Act of 1861'. This railway, latterly the NSR Talke branch, was 2 miles and 32 chains long and ended at the extreme northern end of the site, by the colliery seen on the far right. This photograph shows the scene from the top of the battery of 70 regenerative coke ovens, looking north. From left to right can be seen the by-product recovery plant, the oven retorts, the oven charging gantry, the coal storage bunker and the colliery itself. The whole complex closed in 1928.

Author's collection

Talk o'th Hill Colliery Limited with wagon No 5. and what appears to be a newly painted dumb buffered coke wagon, though the wheels on the wagon look far from new. Notice the extended sides. It was doubtless photographed with the men who built it at Talke, where it is known that extensive engineering shops existed and heavy wagon repairs undertaken. This photograph was possibly taken in 1890, the livery style being typical of that period. The colour would appear to be red oxide with white letters and black shading. The capacity is not visible but 8 tons would be likely.   *Allan Baker collection*

Invincible, an 0-4-0ST at Talk o'th Hill Colliery c1910. It was built in 1885 and saw earlier service at Bunkers Hill Colliery, Talke.
Manifold collection

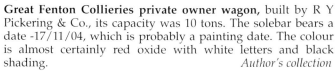

Great Fenton Collieries private owner wagon, built by R Y Pickering & Co., its capacity was 10 tons. The solebar bears a date -17/11/04, which is probably a painting date. The colour is almost certainly red oxide with white letters and black shading.   *Author's collection*

Florence Colliery March 1912, was one of the most up to date of the North Staffordshire collieries. It was owned by the local Shelton Iron, Steel & Coal Company and dated from 1874 - it took its name from the 3rd Duke of Sutherland's eldest daughter, as he was the original owner of the pit. This is a view looking west, showing, from left to right, the headgears of the Nos 1, 2 and 3 shafts. Latterly the workings here were connected to nearby Hem Heath, where all the coal was brought to the surface but, until July 1980, the pit was served by a 2^{1}/3 mile private branch railway connecting with the main line at Trentham. *G Fisher collection*

The Etruria Mills of Shelton Iron & Steel Works 1890, with the iron pudding furnaces in a semi circle in the middle of the photograph and the wrought iron rolling mills behind. The view looks east, the furnaces and mills standing on the site later occupied by the 36" rolling mills, only recently demolished. The Trent & Mersey canal passes behind the mill buildings. Notice the old Beyer Peacock locomotive peeping from behind the weighbridge building, the piles of pig iron to the left in front of the furnaces, and the piles of coke and limestone. The dumb buffered wagons are also of interest. *Keele University Library Warrilow collection*

Shelton Iron & Steel Works 1890, another view, this time showing the other furnaces and mills of the Shelton Company, at Shelton itself, and taken from Hanley looking west towards Etruria. The furnaces are to the left and the mills in the centre. The narrow gauge railway is interesting, apparently serving the coke stocking ground, the coke ovens being behind the photographer. This site was later occupied by the 18" rolling mill, and Etruria Road is just off the picture to the extreme left. The house roofs that can just be discerned would be on the opposite side of the road, then known as Mill Street in view of its proximity to these mills.

Keele University Library Warrilow collection

Below: Shelton Works 23 June 1917, showing the newly built weighbridge at the north end of the coking plant. The wagons in the background contained coal for the coke ovens. The large house visible in the left background stood overlooking the junction of the canal with the Middleport branch, and was standing in the Thirties. Right on the junction was a boatyard, where canal boats were built and repaired, as well as the Anderton boatyard, which was covered, further along the canal towards Longport. *Author's collection*

Blast Furnaces at Shelton 23 November 1916, a view showing the base of the blast furnaces, apparently being tapped. The furnace itself is the circular structure to the right, with its adjacent hot blast stove to the left - the latter used the waste heat from the furnace to heat the incoming blast air. The rail mounted ladles were used to take molten metal to the soaking pits prior to the steel furnaces, or slag to the tipping grounds. *Author's collection*

Glenalmond, **an 0-4-0 saddle tank,** seen here when new, was the fourth and last locomotive built by the Shelton Iron, Steel & Coal Company for their own use. Based on existing engines in their fleet built by the Kilmarnock based Andrew Barclay Company, the engine was totally built in the Shelton shops, except for the boiler which came from nearby W G Bagnall Company Ltd. of Stafford. Notice the lovely finish, the engine taking its name from the Scottish seat in Strathallan, Perthshire, of the Chairman of the Company, Lord Faringdon. *Glenalmond* was one of the last steam locomotives to operate on the Shelton complex, lasting until February 1972, although out of use for a couple of years prior to that date. *Author's collection*

The two Rowhurst Pits of the Shelton Iron and Steel Company were situated on the site later occupied by westward extensions to Hanley Goods Yard. This is the No 2 shaft in a photograph taken in 1891; it was the downcast shaft, 1554 feet deep. Notice the battery of boilers in the foreground, the primitive winding engine house and the dumb buffered wagons. These pits closed in 1908, when developments at Deep Pit took over the underground operations. They were reached by a standard gauge railway connection from the main works site, that passed under the Loop Line south of Hanley Junction. *British Steel Corporation collection*

Deep Pit Hanley c1912, so named because at one time it had the deepest shafts in the locality, dated from 1874 and was connected to the parent Shelton Iron & Steel Works by an internal standard gauge railway dating from 1898-9. Much modernised in 1907-8, this photograph was doubtless taken to show the new surface installations. Notice the Shelton private owner wagons, the piles of wooden pit props and the varied selection of wagons. The pit passed to the NCB on nationalisation of the coal industry in 1947 and closed in 1962. This view looks north, with the upcast shaft headgear to the left, (notice the airlock within the headsticks) and the downcast to the right. *Author's collection*

Alexander, **an 0-4-0T,** built by W C Bagnall of Stafford in 1892, had many years of service at Birchenwood Colliery before being scrapped. Note the wonderful herringbone pattern polished onto its sides with oily rags. *Allan Baker collection*

Nettlebank Wharf c1905. Robert Heath built a private railway from his Norton Colliery to serve a local landsale wharf on the High Lane at Nettlebank; it opened in 1892 and closed on 1 May 1953. To gain the necessary height, a zig-zag arrangement was utilised. Here, one of the Robert Heath built 0-4-0ST's descends from the wharf with empties for the colliery.

Chatterley Whitfield Mining Museum

BIDDULPH VALLEY IRONWORKS.

B.228.

Biddulph Valley Ironworks c1905, a view looking north west, with the NSR Biddulph Valley line in a cutting behind the works and Biddulph itself out of sight to the right. On the left are the blast furnaces and iron works, and on the right the adjacent collieries. Part of Robert Heath's empire. The Heath's were large and influential local industrialists and land owners, and this plant dates from 1860. Heath was influential in the construction of the Biddulph Valley railway, obviously essential to serve these then projected operations. The Ironworks closed in 1929 but the pits survived as Victoria Colliery until 1982. *Keele University Library Warrilow collection*

Chatterley Whitfield 8 September 1874, showing Middle Pit, sunk in 1863 and so named as it lay between Engine Pit, to its south west and also dating from 1863, and Institute Pit to the north east. Prior to the sinking of the latter, the Middle Pit was known as Ragman Pit, as it was sunk to mine the coal seam of that name. The shaft was 450ft deep, was deepened to reach the Hardmine coal at 750ft in 1892 and remained in use until the colliery closed in 1968. This view looks north, with the railway sidings below the bridges in the foreground.

W J Thompson collection

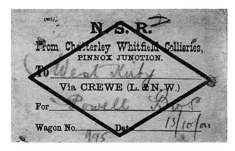

Chatterley Whitfield Colliery looking west 1905. This was the largest colliery site in North Staffordshire, and the only pit in the coalfield to draw in excess of one million tons of coal in private ownership days - it also had one of the largest dirt tips in the country, which could be seen for miles around. It dated from 1863 in its later form but there had been earlier smaller operat-ions on the site. From left to right are the headgears of Middle Pit (1863), Institute Pit (1863) and Platt Pit (1883). The Great Northern Railway wagons in the foreground would be for locomotive coal supplies for that railway. Notice the Yorkshire Engine Company 0-6-0 saddle tank in the middle; the Colliery had three of these, dating from 1877-81 and they served extremely well, surviving until the 1960s. *W J Thompson collection*

0-4-0ST *Dolly,* **March 1923** at Chatterley Whitfield, was built by the Yorkshire Engine Company in 1891. It was purchased originally for work at Bucknall but came to Whitfield when Ubberley closed in 1904; it returned later to work at Botteslow and was much used on the Whitfield Collier's train (which ran between 1887 and 1930) carrying miners from Burslem and Tunstall to the colliery itself. In later years Chell Halt, on the Biddulph Valley line, was used by this service. *Author's collection*

Milton c1920, looking towards Cheadle showing the changing industrial landscape in the foreground. Bullers were electrical porcelain manufacturers, with works at Hanley and at Milton. Just beyond Bullers' works can be seen the Leek branch, with a goods train barely visible. Across the centre of the picture can be seen the Caldon Canal. The railway at Milton saw considerable freight activity, with the British Aluminium Company, Hardman's Chemical Works and Bullers' all having sidings. *Author's collection*

Leek and Moorlands Co-operative Society private owner wagon, built by Hurst Nelson, here recorded in photographic grey. *Author's collection*

Bosley c1909; two views of the industrial tramroad of 2' 6" gauge which connected the wharf on the Macclesfield Canal with the flour and corn mill of F R Thompstone and Sons. This firm was dissatisfied with the service that they were getting from the NSR and constructed the tramroad in the summer of 1887. The first engine to work the half mile line was *Magnet I,* acquired from W G Bagnall of Stafford in 1887 at a cost of £292 10s. This was replaced in the summer of 1909 by *Magnet II,* also from Bagnalls, at a cost of £315. The tramroad remained in use until c1925 and *Magnet II* then saw further service at Cralloch Allison & Co., (Eaglescliffe, County Durham).The **top** photograph from the embankment of the Churnet Valley line looks down towards Lowerworks Mill, the line skirting round the houses in the centre foreground. There was a passing point coming out to the right of Harrington House, in the centre background, where the tramroad crossed the road to run alongside the works. The **bottom** photograph is taken from near Bosley NSR level crossing, looking towards the Macclesfield Canal. Far left can be seen the rear of *Magnet II* and the wagon that carried the corn, behind which is Thompstone's warehouse; immediately behind can be seen the tramroad with the work's cottages on the left hand side. Top: *G Bowyer collection* Bottom: *Author's collection*

Froghall Works of Thomas Bolton & Sons c1905, looking towards Caldon. The Churnet Valley line can be seen bottom, with the original Bolton's Sidings signal box just visible in the centre. On the left is the Bolt Mill, built in 1900, and in the centre is the older Electro Refining Strip Mill, the first building on the new Froghall site, erected in 1890. *Author's collection*

Dunkirk Quarry Caldon Low c1905, looking towards Ashbourne. In the foreground is the main tramroad leading to the incline. Note the other tramroads at right angles to the main line. These went up the quarry face, where stone was loaded into the wagons, each wagon capable of holding six tons. A workman's hut can be seen centre left. This large quarry face was one of several worked by the NSR, which obtained its interest in the quarry as a result of its acquisition of the Trent and Mersey Canal in 1846. The limestone hill of Caldon Low, between Ashbourne and Leek, had been quarried by various family interests in the 18th century and, in 1769, the proprietors of the Trent and Mersey Canal obtained a 999 year lease to work the quarry. Expansion of output occurred from the late 1860's, when the quarry was more intensively worked through the increased employment of specialist miners recruited from Bangor and Anglesey, and this recruitment continued until 1902. Upwards of 200,000 tons of limestone was quarried each year, and when Dunkirk and other quarries near the Ashbourne Road were worked out, new quarry workings were established lower down the hill, from around 1903. These were served by the NSR's Leek to Caldon and Waterhouses branch. In 1902, before the new quarry was opened, approximately 310 people worked in the older quarries. *Author's collection*

Caldon Low locomotive shed c1900, looking towards Oakamoor with the Ashbourne road in the background. In the foreground are 3' 6" gauge 0-4-0 saddle tank locomotives, *Frog* on the left and *Toad* on the right. Both these locomotives were built by H Hughes & Co. in 1877 and worked the 3' 6" tramways - transporting the dynamited limestone from near the quarry face to the incline, from which it descended by cable tramway to Froghall Wharf. Behind the locomotives is the timber engine shed, also built in 1877, to the right of which can be seen the crudely constructed water tank. The engine shed was enlarged in 1901, following the purchase from Bagnall's of another 0-4-0ST *Bobs*, with the right hand side being extended outwards. To the left of the engine shed is a collection of small workshops - for the blacksmiths and the wagon repairers - as well as stables for the shunting horses and two workmen's cottages.

Finney-Elks collection

Oakamoor c1905 looking west, showing part of the works complex of Thomas Bolton & Sons, manufacturers of copper, brass and bronze products, whilst in the immediate foreground can be seen the two brick kilns of Elijah Bottom & Sons, who owned a firebrick and clay works. Behind the kilns is the Tube Department, known as "The Meadow", which was built in 1894. Far left can be seen the 'Wing' line to Oakamoor station, to the right of which can be seen the Bronze Wire Mill and then the Hard Wire Mill (built in 1885) and the Bolt Mill (built in 1887). Thomas Patten established a brass works at Cheadle and a brass-wire mill at Alton in 1734, and a copper and brass mill at Oakamoor in 1792; this mill was sold to Thomas Bolton for £7750 in 1852. The Oakamoor works employed 600 people in 1905. *Author's collection*

Fauld c1892, where J C Staton & Co. owned gypsum mines. The two 0-4-0 saddle tank locomotives were built by Bagnall's of Stafford, the leading locomotive arriving in 1891, whilst the trailing locomotive was delivered in January 1889 for the opening of the 3' gauge tramway. Staton's drift mine at Fauld opened in 1879. There were five trips daily from Fauld to the NSR exchange sidings at Scropton, where stone was transshipped to Staton's standard gauge wagons and then worked forward three miles to Staton's plaster mills at Tutbury. Staton's had an engine shed at Scropton and their locomotives and wagons were painted madder lake. *Allan Baker/Allen Civil collection*

CANALS

Shardlow looking east c1910, with the sheds on the left and a steam boat, perhaps an inspection launch, centre right. Shardlow was an inland port conveniently near the junction of the Trent and Mersey Canal and the River Trent, and handled the interchange of goods between canal and river craft. It was also conveniently situated on the main Derby to Loughborough road. Authority to construct the canal came from the Trent and Mersey Act of 1766. The canal was opened progressively from October 1772 to May 1777 and went from Derwent Mouth, near Shardlow, to Preston Brook, near Runcorn, a distance of 93⅜ miles.   *Author's collection*

Bottom Lock Stone c1910, with the headquarters of the Trent and Mersey Canal on the right. Also to the right can be seen NSR engineer's boat No. 33, with limestone chatter (small broken stone) on the footpath. The building on the left is a toll house, beyond which can be seen the bridge carrying the A520 over the canal and Bottom Lock itself, to the left of which is to be found the Star public house. In the background can be seen two gas holders.   *Author's collection*

***Dolly Varden* c1905,** the NSR inspection launch on the Trent and Mersey Canal, outside the wheelwright's shop of the NSR Carriage and Wagon Works. The wagon maker's shop is in the background and a three-plank wagon for loco coal can just be seen. The *Dolly Varden* was built in the 1860s and in the centre of the cabin panels can be seen the NSR crest. *Author's collection*

Shelton 23 May 1917, looking north and showing the construction of the bridge to carry an elevated railway serving the new blast furnace bunkers. This provides a fine view of the building techniques. Just beneath the bridge a wide boat is being used to transport bricks for the bridge.

Author's collection

Shelton 3 September 1917, with the chimneys of Shelton Iron and Steel Works in the background and the Trent and Mersey Canal snaking under the newly constructed railway bridge. The line it carried connected with the Grange branch of the NSR. Note the new earthworks on either side of the bridge and four Shelton private owner wagons. On the left is the cooling tower, beside which is the old bridge linking the two parts of Shelton works. *Author's collection*

Middleport 1910 looking south. A typical canal side picture of pot banks and works, which stretched along the banks of the Trent and Mersey Canal for many years.
Author's collection

The northern end of the two Harecastle Tunnels, looking south 1907. On the right is the original tunnel, designed by James Brindley. 2880 yards long, it took nine years to build and was opened for traffic in September 1775. This tunnel was the first transport tunnel in England and the longest ever attempted. It was abandoned in 1918 having become a bottleneck due to the growth in traffic. A second tunnel, 2936 yards long, designed by Thomas Telford, was built between 1825 and 1827 and this can be seen on the left hand side; this tunnel was later electrified and electric tugs were purchased and introduced in November 1914. In the centre foreground is *Westwood*, owned by J & G Meakin, potters of Hanley, which was used to carry pottery. On the towpath is the young assistant of Harrison of Newcastle, the photographer, who was commissioned by the NSR to take this and other photographs for inclusion in an Illustrated Guide Book produced in 1908. Immediately behind is the NSR Engineer's Department boat No. 44, and stacked against the wall between the two tunnels are various materials belonging to the Engineer's Department.
Mrs W J Brown collection

Harecastle Tunnel c 1910, looking north. A view taken from the original Brindley tunnel, with the mouth of the second or Telford tunnel on the right. In the foreground is the NSR Engineer's Department boat, equipped with crane, based at nearby Lawton, to the north. In the background is the turnover bridge and immediately behind is the mainline from Harecastle to Stoke. *Author's collection*

Harecastle c1910, looking towards the two tunnels in the background. On the left can be seen a Robert Heath locomotive propelling wagons along the Bathpool sidings towards Birchenwood Colliery. On the right of the canal is the coal drop with a 5-ton crane engaged in transhipping coal brought from the Settle Speakman Colliery at Alsager, into the narrow boats queuing up. Several horses take a well earned rest. In the centre of the picture are two down distant signals for the lines to Crewe and Macclesfield and behind the crane is the Harecastle Junction signal box.

Author's collection

Big Lock Middlewich c1905, looking south with the milk factory in the background. In the foreground is *Lily,* from Northwich, with a load of wooden crates.
Author's collection

The Anderton Lift 1884, owned by the Weaver Navigation Trustees. It connected the River Weaver and the Trent and Mersey Canal. Designed by Edwin Clark the lift, built at a cost of £48,000, was opened in 1875 and consisted of two tanks or caissons, supported on hydraulics in equilibrium; so one tank was always up and the other down. The tanks were designed to accommodate two narrow boats or one large barge of up to 100 tons. The engine house is in the centre with the newly built chimney on the right.
National Trust collection

The Anderton Lift c1920 after its rebuilding between 1906 and 1908. The original boilers were found to be unsafe in 1902 so in 1903 steam was replaced by electricity and, by 1908, the hydraulic system had been replaced by counterbalance weights. These alterations made the transit of boats a more rapid process as well as reducing power and labour costs. *Author's collection*

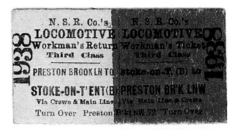

Barnton Tunnel c1905, looking west. 572 yards long, the Barnton tunnel, like those at Saltersford and Preston Brook, also used steam tugs, introduced in 1864 and 1865. The boat in the foreground is *Nellie*. *Author's collection*

Preston Brook 1905, looking south, the canal in the foreground being the Preston Brook branch of the Bridgewater Canal. It connects a few hundred yards to the south with the Trent and Mersey Canal, at the north end of the 1239 yards long Preston Brook tunnel. The house to the left belonged to the Manchester Ship Canal Company and the one beyond to the NSR. The large warehouse building to the right was used jointly by the Trent and Mersey Canal and the Manchester Ship Canal. Several narrow boats, a crane and warehousemen complete this delightful scene. *Cheshire County Council Museum Service*

Brickworks Hanley c1905, with the Caldon Canal snaking eastwards towards Lichfield Street. *Author's collection*

Planet Lock on the Caldon Canal Stoke on Trent 1909. This lock was built in 1909 and on the right can be seen W D Phillipps, General Manager of the NSR, sitting on a narrow boat at the official opening. In the background is the outline of the tall Trent & Mersey Canal warehouse at Cauldon Place. The lock was named after *Planet*, the first boat to pass through it

Ellesmere Port Boat Museum

Stockton Brook c1920, looking towards Etruria, with the basin into the Staffordshire Potteries Waterworks just visible on the right.
Author's collection

Willow Cottage Bridge near Cheddleton c1905, looking towards Froghall, with a loaded limestone boat being hauled towards Etruria.
Author's collection

Froghall Tunnel west end c1905, looking towards Froghall Basin, with a boat being legged through the short 76 yards tunnel, carrying about twenty tons of broken limestone. This section was not part of the original canal works as opened in 1778 but formed part of a 530 yards extension completed in 1785. Above the tunnel can be seen advertisements for the *Weekly Sentinel* and the Leek United Building Society, pasted on the stables of the Navigation Hotel, or 'The Navvy' as it was known locally. The stables provided accommodation for eight canal horses.   *R Cartwright collection*

First pound of the former Uttoxeter Canal at Froghall 1905, with Primrose Thorley, partner in Bowers & Thorley, at the helm of *Farmer's Friend*, one of several boats used by this firm of lime burners, who were based at Froghall. In the background is a former warehouse building.
                                                                                               Author's collection

Froghall Basin c1904, looking towards the limestone business of Thorley and Bowers. This is a superb view of lime burning and limestone loading, showing smoke creeping across the valley and polluting the working environment of the limestone crushers and loaders alike. The narrow boat in the foreground, named *Bear*, belongs to Brunner Mond & Co. (forerunners of ICI), of Winnington and Sandbach, whilst on the far right another narrow boat is being loaded. The buildings are, from left to right, the Stores (just visible) Workmen's Mess, Weigh Cabin, Offices (with the middle one occupied by the Goods Agent), the sheds where lime was burnt, Primrose Thorley's office and, on the right of the Foxt road, can be seen George Mosley's corn warehouse.

R Cartwright collection

NORTH STAFFORDSHIRE RAILWAY.

NOTICE.

THE North Staffordshire Railway Company hereby give Public Notice, that the portion of the Cauldon Canal, extending from FROGHALL to UTTOXETER, will be permanently CLOSED, on and after Monday, the 15th of JANUARY next. Railway Office, Stoke, Dec. 29, 1848.

Closure notice of the Uttoxeter Canal, issued by the NSR in December 1848. The Uttoxeter canal was opened in September 1811 and went from Froghall to Uttoxeter, a distance of 13$^{1/4}$ miles; it never attracted much traffic. It was used to convey materials for the construction of the Churnet Valley line and part of the railway track was laid on the canal bed in locations between Froghall and Rocester. *Author's collection*

Leek Branch of the Caldon Canal c1905. This is a view of the Horse Bridge, looking west. This branch was 2$^{3/4}$ miles long and was opened in 1801. Although it carried little traffic, it was not finally abandoned until the London, Midland & Scottish Railway Act of 1944 was passed.
G Bowyer collection

Leek branch near Hollinshay Woods c1905, and a delightful Edwardian fishing scene.

G Bowyer collection

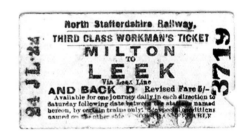

Leek Canal basin c1900, with the warehouse in the foreground plus a narrow boat and crane in view. Behind is the Goods Office. In the background, left, can be seen the water tower on the down platform of Leek station, in front of which are several 5-plank wagons.

L Porter collection

Newcastle Canal c1900, with a view of The Villas in the left background. Note the highly ornate nature of the footbridge.

Author's collection

Newcastle-under-Lyme Canal at Station Road, Stoke c1920, looking northwards toward its junction with the Trent & Mersey Canal. To the right is the Newcastle arm, or tunnel, into the flint mill. The Newcastle Canal was completed in 1797 but was acquired by the NSR in 1863. The canal remained in use for the remainder of the 19th century, although the onward trade to Newcastle was insignificant. The canal was abandoned and filled in as far as Aqueduct Street by 1938.

Author's collection

MISCELLANY

Rudyard Lake 1868, looking north-east. A view taken from the green at the end of the dam, looking across to the Earl of Macclesfield's boathouse. Behind the boathouse, hidden by the trees, ran the Churnet Valley line between Macclesfield and Leek. Until the 1890s there were very few boathouses on the Lake. The attractions of water and scenery led to an increasing number of industrialists from the Potteries coming to live in Rudyard and building their own boathouses there, whilst a few of Leek industrialists did likewise. *Author's collection*

Rudyard Hotel 1868, one of the earliest photographs of the Rudyard area to have survived. The building in the foreground was the water bailiff's house, built and owned by the Trent and Mersey Canal Company for the original Rudyard reservoir, which Company was acquired by the NSR in 1846. This house was licensed to sell ale in August 1850 but it became clear that, with the growing attraction of visitors to Rudyard Lake from Manchester, the Potteries and the Midlands, a hotel was needed. Additional accommodation was provided in 1852 and this can be seen in the background. A new house was built for the water bailiff at the same time, overlooking the dam at the south end of the Lake; this still survives and continues to be occupied by the water bailiff. *Author's collection*

Rudyard Lake Hotel 1876, as portrayed on a visiting card used by the hotel proprietor, Henry Platt. In the foreground is an artist's impression of passenger trains approaching each other, behind which yachts and rowing boats can be seen. The Hotel gardens slope down to the Lake. By this time the Hotel has been enlarged as the NSR continued to promote the attractions of the area, despite being denied, by an injunction from the House of Lords dating back to 1856, from utilising the Lake for pleasure purposes. To the left of the Hotel can be seen the stables, whilst on the far right is what is possibly the newly constructed skating rink. *William Salt Library*

Rudyard Lake Golf Links 1906, one of six 'official' postcards published by the NSR to promote the Golf Club and travel to Rudyard Lake. The Club was privately owned and, whilst it leased land from the NSR who owned the Cliffe Park estate, it was heavily supported by the 'Knotty' who for some years paid for the Club's golf professional and for three groundsmen. It opened on 19 April 1906 and was initially a 9 hole course. This is a view from the first tee of the original course; so popular did it become, set as it was amongst idyllic surroundings along the edge of the Lake, that in 1908 it was extended into an 18 hole course. In the background can be seen the first club house for the original course and next to it the tea room; when the course was enlarged, Cliffe Park Hall, also acquired by the NSR, became the new club house. The course had a short life, closing in 1926. *Author's collection*

Market Place, Leek 1912, with an impressive parade of NSR horses and drays. Left to right are Bill Bloor, William Lockett, Harry Fearn, Jack Bray, and Tommy Lathem, with the last gentleman being unidentified, *Author's collection*

Leek station 1905, looking north, with the bowler hatted commuters boarding the train for Macclesfield and Manchester. On the right can be seen a porter loading parcels into a brake third, the inside door of the parcels compartment clearly being painted white. There is also a good view of the parcels trolley in the foreground.

Author's collection

The Black Lion Inn Consall c1905, with the landlord, Edward Currie, and his family outside the pub. The hay and corn warehouse is on the left. The NSR crossing gates are in the foreground and beyond can be seen the Churnet Valley line. Because of its remoteness and lack of road links, ale was delivered in barrels by rail, a practice which continued until the late 1950s

G Bowyer collection

Froghall c1914, looking towards Alton with E class 0-6-0 locomotive No. 112 on ballast duties. The vehicle behind the tender is the NSR Engineer's Ballast Brake Van (to drawing 2200), perhaps the only photograph of the Van to have survived. The ballast gang was a specialist gang in the Permanent Way department, working all over the NSR network. At the time of this photograph the gang consisted of a foreman, Isaac Jackson, in the bowler hat, W Rutter, assistant foreman and approximately 23 labourers. Note the tall water tank on the right and the large number of trolleys.

Jackson family collection

Jimmy's Yard Oakamoor 1905, where a Methodist Sunday school meeting is taking place with the preacher giving his address from a NSR two-plank wagon. Everyone is dressed in their Sunday best. The railway line in the foreground has come off the 'Wing' line from Oakamoor station, passing under the Ashbourne to Cheadle road. The house in the background was a NSR house occupied by the goods agent and the stable to the side was for the three shunting horses used on internal works traffic at Thomas Bolton's.

Author's collection

Churnet platform Uttoxeter 11 October 1890, showing the result of a mineral train from Harecastle running into C class 2-4-0 No.14 and driving it into a Midland Railway milk van at the rear of a train for Ashbourne. This photograph shows some of the debris, the damaged locomotive being derailed and the milk van crushed into the tender. The breakdown crane is in the background, to the left of which can be seen some NSR passenger stock.

Author's collection

Fenton station 1910, looking north towards Stoke with a Sunday school procession travelling down Heron Street, passing the Railway Hotel and crossing the railway by the recently constructed footbridge. The station was remodelled during 1906 and re-opened on 1 November 1906, with the footbridge coming into use on that date and the signal box, which worked the level crossing gates, closing. Heron Street, which crossed the railway line, was blocked off and the level crossing taken out of use. Behind the station can be seen the bottle banks of the Opal China Works, whilst further down Heron Street can be seen a gable end advertising *'The Daily Sentinel*, read by everyone'.

A Priestley collection

Cheadle c1915, with two views of local volunteers of the Staffordshire Regiment leaving the station to fight in the First World War. The **top** view, taken from the platform and looking west towards Tean, shows some thirty soldiers sitting down for a farewell meal.

The **bottom** view shows the large crowds thronging the platform as the train, consisting of Loop Line stock, pulls away for Stoke. The station building was opened on 1 February 1910 at a cost of £1260, replacing the original which had been built for the extension of the railway to Cheadle on 1 January 1901. In the background, behind the passenger stock, can be seen the original goods warehouse and loading gauge, built by the Cheadle Railway, and extended by the NSR in November 1910.

Author's collection

Ashbourne c1898. A view looking north towards Buxton, showing the construction of the tunnel and the trackbed for the railway line, under the Leek to Ashbourne Road and towards the new Ashbourne station. The contractor's line is visible in the foreground.
Foxfield Railway Jack Hollick collection

Ashbourne station c1910; an unusual view of the rear of the timbered station, as the locals enjoy their Shrove Tuesday game of football. Note the bridge which crosses the railway line at the north end of the station, whilst beyond the crowds watching the spectacle from the down platform, can be seen the Station Hotel, opened in 1903.
Author's collection

Ashbourne station 1905, with passengers and station master David Dean on the up platform, standing outside the bookstall of W H Smith & Sons Ltd of 136 The Strand WC – as the advertising board displays. The quality of this postcard view is outstanding and enables an enormous amount of detail to be discerned. Magazines on sale include *Hearth and Hound*, *The Stage*, *Illustrated London News*, *The Graphic*, *Country Life*, *The Garden*, *The Winning Post*, *Black and White*, the *Queen*, and the *King*. A newspaper billboard for the *Manchester Guardian* newspaper announces 'Defeat for the Government, Great Scene. Premier's Attitude'; it is almost possible to identify the local scenes on the many postcards offered for sale. Of railway interest is the L&NWR station design, with its timber cladding, wooden platforms, and characteristic gas lamps. The station clock is made by W Potts & Sons of Leeds. Also clearly to be seen is the advertising board of W & A Gilbey, wine merchants and distributors, whose Ashbourne agents were T Mellor & Sons of Church Street. The station master's hat bears the initials 'AJS' – Ashbourne Joint Station – which was jointly managed by the L&NWR and the NSR.

Author's collection

Steam Traverser Stoke Works c1920, at the rear of the two Carriage Sheds. This traverser rail system was installed around 1908 after the second shed had been built, had three lanes and enabled carriages to be moved out of the sheds towards Pratt Sidings. One shed had two lanes and the other three. In the background can be seen Stoke Basin, with the Trent and Mersey Canal beyond the arch. *Author's collection*

Left: **NSR Breakdown Steam Crane,** seen here at Diglake, having come to grief when attempting to lift a loaded coal wagon which had run down an embankment. The crane was supplied to the NSR by Cowan and Sheldon in 1895, at a cost of £1550. *Manifold collection*

Scropton c1912, with the underbridge being renewed. The NSR had a number of small hand cranes used by the Engineers Department. Two are shown here working at bridge 84. The cranes are a standard design with balance weights and were secured to the rails when operating. Locomotive-type buffers were fitted and the vehicles were braked on one side only. In the foreground, right, is the exchange siding, where alabaster was transshipped from the 3' narrow gauge line which linked the Fauld alabaster mines of J C Staton & Co., 1½ miles away, with the Derby line. *Manifold collection*

NSR Fire Engine *Merryweather* **c1910,** can be seen here outside the NSR Stores department. On the left is Charles Bentley, the Captain. and second left is William Peake. It was named after the London company which supplied it. *Dow family collection*

A drowning incident at Great Haywood on 9 March 1905 led to a search for the body of the niece of Mrs Challenor, the wife of the town Clerk of Hanley. The body was not found immediately and this led to a further search which required the River Trent to be diverted. To achieve this, fire engines from all over Staffordshire were called in to pump out water. In the centre of the picture, second on the left, can be seen the NSR engine hard at work. *Author's collection*

North Stafford Hotel c1920. A rear view taken from the fishing pool, with houses for the officers of the NSR clearly visible on the left. The Hotel was opened in June 1849 and built at a cost of £1900; it became so well patronised that it was enlarged in 1878 and was later referred to as the Five Towns Hotel in an Arnold Bennett novel. It was let to various tenants down to 1918, when it was leased to the Home Counties Public House Trust for a 14 year term. It was the best appointed Hotel in the Potteries with, for example, a Smoke Room, a Commercial Room, a Coffee Room, a Reading and Waiting Room, an Arbitration or Meeting Room, a Billiard Room and a Banqueting Room.   *National Monuments Record*

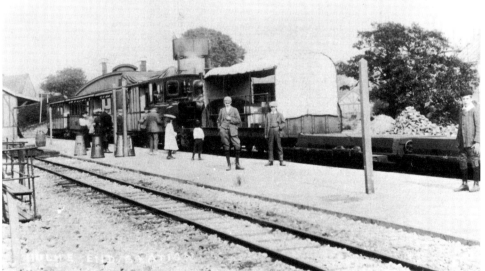

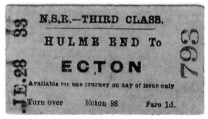

Hulme End station July 1904, shortly after the station opened, with bricks and ballast in the background. The station building is partially visible on the left, whilst foreground left are the enclosed rails and passenger benches which were used for the opening day celebrations on 29 June 1904. This station was one of several on the separately owned Leek and Manifold Light Railway, a 2' 6" gauge system which ran between Waterhouses and Hulme End. The NSR operated the line on behalf of the Light Railway Company. Note the lightly ballasted track in the foreground and the new platform, only slightly elevated above the trackbed. Near the milk churns can be seen the rear of the station name board, and then the train itself - three passenger carriages, the locomotive, an open wagon (converted into passenger stock by fitting knifeboard seats and iron hoops to carry a canopy roof), and two transporters. Behind the carriages is the two lane engine shed, to the right of which can just be seen the water tower. Not visible, behind the converted open wagon, is the two lane carriage shed.   *G Fisher collection*

Hulme End July 1904, with 2-6-4T locomotive No. 1, *E J Calthrop,* freshly out of shops and in immaculate condition. The locomotive's design was based on a class supplied to the Barsi Light Railway in India. It weighed 26 tons 16 cwt. and was 29' 2" in length with driving wheels which were 2' 6" in diameter. In the background, left, can be seen two narrow gauge transporter wagons to enable transshipment of wagons to and from the narrow gauge line at Waterhouses; there were standard gauge sidings at several Manifold stations - Sparrowlee, Grindon, Wetton Mill, Butterton, Ecton and Hulme End. *Author's collection*

Darfur Crags, Manifold Valley 1905, as one of two locomotives of the Leek and Manifold Valley Light Railway heads a 3rd class carriage and 1st/3rd brake composite between Butterton and Wetton Mill. The 3rd class carriage could hold 44 passengers, whilst the composite could carry eight 1st class and twenty-two 2nd class passengers. *Author's collection*

Redhurst 1904, with driver and fireman posing, whilst on the Waterhouses to Hulme End working. The locomotive is *J B Earle*, seen here in NSR madder lake livery, one of two 2-6-4 Tank locomotives built by Kitson & Co and delivered to the separate Leek and Manifold Valley Light Railway Company in May and June 1904, in advance of the 8¼ mile line opening on 29 June 1904. *J B Earle*, No. 2, arrived in May and was withdrawn from service at Crewe on 23 February 1935, approximately eleven months after the line was closed on 12 March 1934, being scrapped in May 1937. The passenger carriage is one of two primrose yellow 1st/3rd brake composites built by the Electric Railway & Tramway Carriage Works Ltd, of Preston, the forerunners of the English Electric Company. All around is evidence of 'newness' - the limestone-reinforced embankments, the fencing, the bridge and buttresses over the River Manifold, and the newly made paths. To the left but just off the picture, is the location of Redhurst Crossing, a passenger station with a milk loading platform; the milk platform came into use in 1910 and the passenger station in the summer of 1915.
Author's collection

Thor's Cave station summer 1904, as the line sweeps tightly to the right. The station building was, in effect, a waiting room, one of several of similar design on the line, each built by the Portable Building Company of Fleetwood at a cost of £40. To the left, just visible, was the original tea room at Thor's Cave, soon to be replaced by a larger tea room, capable of accommodating more easily the growing numbers visiting the Manifold Valley. Again, notice the low platform and light ballast. *Author's collection*

Beeston Tor station 1906, with, in the foreground right, the station platform and waiting room - a redundant NSR four compartment railway carriage. Just visible through the branches of the tree in the foreground is the Beeston Tor tearoom, to the left of which is a hut, probably with facilities to enable trippers to boil water for their tea. *G Fisher collection*

NSR Steam Bus 1904, seen here outside the Plough Hotel at Endon. This bus was one of two purchased from Straker & Co of Bristol, one at the price of £45 and the other costing £60, in the summer of 1904. This was in order to provide a road link between Leek and Waterhouses to connect with the then newly opened Manifold Valley line. Delays in the completion of the railway line from Leek to Waterhouses, mainly caused by bad weather and land slippages, meant that the NSR felt under an obligation to provide this road link, until the line opened on 1 July 1905. The road journey for the seven miles from Leek to Waterhouses took 40 minutes and there were four journeys per day each way; the bus held 22 passengers and had a roof rack, as this picture clearly shows. The cost of the double journey, Leek to Waterhouses by road and Waterhouses to Hulme End and return, was 3/-. The bus had iron tyred wheels, which caused considerable damage to roads in Leek. The circumstances behind this particular photograph are not clear, because Endon was away from its normal run; maybe it was on a proving run between Stoke and Leek, before coming into service. *Author's collection*